AF324373

HOW BELIEF STORIES MATTER

Other Books By The Author

Speaking of Rhetoric
(co-editor)
Houghton Mifflin

Eugene O'Neill in China
(contributor)
Greenwood Press

World Without Heroes:
The Brooklyn Novels of Daniel Fuchs
Fairleigh-Dickinson University Press

The Romance of Elsewhere:
A Half Century of Connecting
By Sea, By Air, By Rail
Regent Press

HOW BELIEF STORIES MATTER

An Approach to Myth

by

Marcelline Krafchick, Ph.D.

REGENT PRESS
Berkeley, California

ISBN-13: 978-1-58790-202-4
ISBN-10: 1-58790-202-8
Library of Congress Control Number: 2009944182

www.MarcellineKrafchick.com

Manufactured in the U.S.A.
REGENT PRESS
www.regentpress.net

For those students
who have remained
my life-long friends

HOW BELIEF STORIES MATTER

Table of Contents

Preface

Miriam Robbins Dexter

ONE PERSON'S myth is another's religion—and vice-versa—and thus one would expect comparative mythologists to study myth-making and the myth-makers of all cultures with the respect due a deep belief-system. However, in the past, many mythologists, as well as anthropologists, treated the belief-systems of most non-western religions as somehow not civilized. Marcelline Krafchick, to my delight, honestly and respectfully relates belief stories from peoples around the world. She writes of Hindu, Jain, Muslim, Christian, Jew, Miwok, Paraguayan Lengua, the Winnebago of Wisconsin, Oregon's Klamath Yurok tribe, the Inuit of the Arctic and subarctic. She tells stories about Moses, Buddha, Coyote, Krishna, Raven, Jesus, Mohammad, Hindu Vishnu, Greek Demeter, Akkadian/Babylonian Ishtar, and Hittite Telepinu. Dr. Krafchick does not pass judgment on the stories; instead, she respects them as whole entities in themselves, with their own reasons for being. The stories come forth from her pages as rich and nuanced, instead of narrow and stereotyped. Says Krafchick, "When we look at belief stories, however, as an integral element of religions, we rescue them from trivializing and come to appreciate their crucial role." Earlier authors of myth books, such as Thomas Bullfinch and Edith Hamilton, were restricted by the rather narrow anthropological visions of their day, and, as Krafchick tells us, they "conveyed the quaintness of the tales with condescension while eviscerating them of their sacred content." Thus Krafchick understands the sacrality of myth.

Sacred content is at the heart of myth, which deals with the divine, the origins of the cosmos, and other phenomena which represent the truths fundamental to the life of a people. This original meaning of myth stands at opposition to what our news media presents to us today: that myths are falsehoods. For example, a recent flyer for a gourmet food chain advertises that there is a "myth that's been circulating lately . . . if you want to eat on a budget, you have to cut corners. Wrong!" Thus, in modern parlance myths are falsehoods which must be disproved.

Professor Krafchick is a scholar who can make distinctions, and she presents most welcome complexly nuanced definitions of religion, cult, ritual, story, etiology, folklore, legend, myth. On the last, the focus of her book: ". . . myth is the story part of a belief-system." Her communication to us is precise, and because of that we learn a great deal about myth, myth-making, and the societies which make these myths. We learn of heroism and superstition, danger, disaster, joy, and sorrow: the stuff of myths and the stuff of life.

Professor Krafchick demonstrates her in-depth knowledge of myth and folktale when she discusses Homer's tale of Circe, who changes Odysseus' men into beasts. (She also discusses other folkloristic motifs found in the *Odyssey* —obviously a work she has treasured, and taught over and over again.) Krafchick powerfully discusses this tale of "folklore and magic," regarding Circe with far more objectivity than most critics ancient or modern. We learn that Circe, far from being a predatory temptress, is "mentor, nurturer, harmonizer." Not only does Circe not harm Odysseus—and, indeed, she restores Odysseus' men to super-anthropomorphic glory—she gives him careful advice on how best to find his way home to Ithaca. In keeping with Classical tradition, Circe is an excellent host.

Although Homer's tale is one of "literary myth," Circe indeed has roots in the realm of the gods. Like her niece Medea (although without the sadness of Medea's personal story), Circe has the knowledge of *pharmaka*: herbs, medicines, and with them, spells. Because of this she has been thought of as a witch, but she actually has the powers of a goddess, a "mistress of animals," the sort of female figure depicted in so many prehistoric and early historic images. In fact, Circe's lineage is divine: her father was Helios, god of the sun, and her mother was an Oceanid, Perse. In *Odyssey* XII.155 Odysseus calls her a "heavenly one among the goddesses," *dia theaon.* And Odysseus is not just indulging in hyperbole; Krafchick reminds us that Circe even sends a favorable breeze for Odysseus' voyage!

Interleaved among these pages are discussions of John Wayne, Aldous Huxley, Carl Jung, William Butler Yeats, Plato, and Mircea Eliade. Krafchick's lifetime of studying literature and myth is distilled into these brilliant and lovely pages. In addition to imparting much useful knowledge about myth and myths, Krafchick writes with clarity and beauty, breadth of knowledge, concise intellect, wit and wisdom. It is clear that she has thoroughly enjoyed her decades-long romance with myth and story: "the storyteller and listener can enjoy the language that weaves the story . . .

they savor the words." Indeed, so does Krafchick savor the words, as will we when we read her delightful weavings.

Dr. Miriam Robbins Dexter taught courses in Latin, Greek, and Sanskrit language and literature in the Department of Classics at the University of Southern California for thirteen years and has taught for the past twelve in the Women's Studies Department at UCLA. She is the author of Whence the Goddesses: A Source Book *(1990, Pergamon) and more than twenty scholarly articles and nine encyclopedia articles on ancient female figures. She has edited thirteen books on archaeology, linguistics, and myth and co-authored* Sacred Display: Divine and Magical Female Figures of Eurasia *(2010, Cambria Press).*

Model

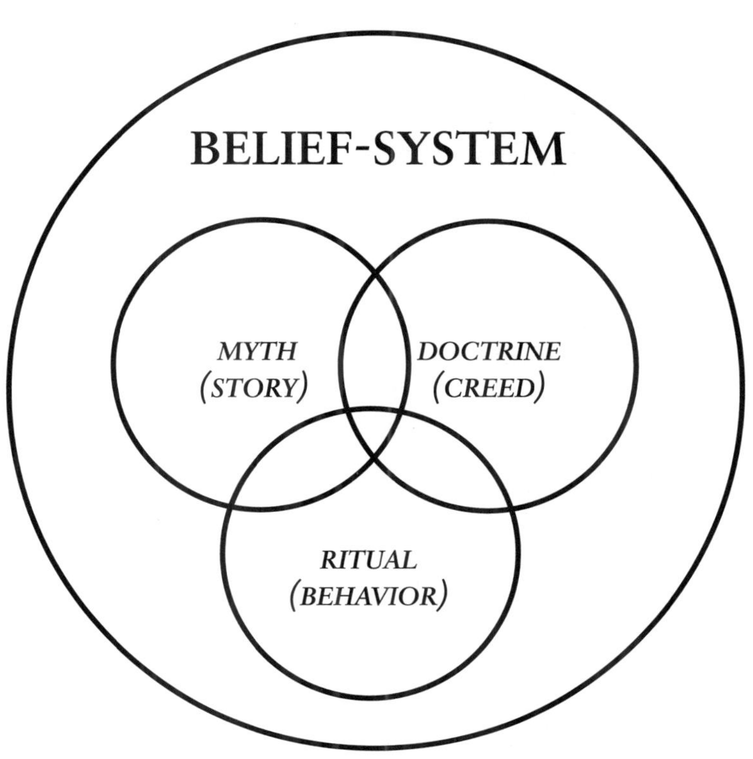

Introduction

A WRITER setting out to produce a book begins with the notion that someone would want to read it, or, better still, needs it. I hope that instructors of mythology courses and general readers outside academe who are curious about the subject are seeking what I've been seeking. Although books about mythology have proliferated in recent years, I have not found one to serve my courses on the subject. What I have sought is a short companion to a range of primary sources like the *Gilgamesh Epic,* African creation tales, and the *Iliad.* That book would offer focus, perspective, and ways to organize insights. Through three decades of teaching university courses on the subject, I would have welcomed such a guide.

A chief aim of this book, then, a distillation of those years of teaching, is to liberate readers from limitation to any particular group of myths—historically the classical stories. My guess as I thought of putting together the book was that an instructor who wants to deal with any number and combination of myths from various cultures, including but not limited to the Greeks, is likely to welcome a means to approach them. The ideas this book advances apply to belief stories from any region with any theme, on the Greeks and Egyptians, or the Chinese and the Aztecs, on heroes' journeys or women and nature.

Unfortunately, many books have been so encyclopedic as to deaden the excitement of myths. They present the lives of mythical characters as biographies, forcing an impression of coherence on their behavior. For example, portrayals of Medea in literature before and after Euripides' popular play by that name are either neutral or benign, yet that playwright's murderous image dominates. She is, after all, a character crafted to fit the different narrative situations in which she appears, in Greek and Roman culture. But she becomes melded into one puzzling personality by writers like Edith Hamilton, whose priority, to her credit, was to popularize. Praise for Hamilton's work, introducing *Mythology*, includes this comment: "She has blended and organized the sometimes conflicting myths of the early storytellers, molding them with vivid clarity" (frontispiece). Robert Graves, in *The Greek Myths*, continues the tradition in more than seven hundred pages of dry narrative with prodigious notes, drawing here from Apollodorus, there from Ovid, here from Thucydides, there from Hesiod, to patch together a two-volume saga summary.

Mythology is both a very easy and a very difficult subject to teach. It is easy because it touches on everything in our lives—music, astronomy, medicine—and because people seem to find it alluring. At the same time it is difficult in that it is vast and unwieldy, susceptible to sloppy and not very fruitful musings. Origins of myths and the belief-systems they nurture are by their nature obscure, having occurred over great periods of time long before they were written down or written about. Collectors and translators with earnest intentions can be expected to be unreliable, and cultural chauvinism can distort foreign-seeming material. Some belief-systems, like Hinduism, for example, can be so complex and daunting that it is difficult to avoid misrepresenting them.

Hinduism is often cited as the prime example of polytheism. After all, its stories, paintings, and temple art deal with a great many deities. Hindu scripture contains no prohibition like that in the second of the Hebrew commandments, against rendering images of the deity, and one finds temple exteriors covered completely with colorful friezes of immortal activities. But the Supreme Brahman is at the center of all Hindu worship, immutable, existence itself, without beginning or ending, neither inside nor outside, ultimately indescribable. The multiple gods who people the many tales and temples are to be seen as versions, sub-versions, and manifestations, with such weighty responsibilities as creation (Brahma), preservation (Vishnu), and dissolution (Shiva). (Brahmin, a similar name, denotes the highest of the four castes.)

Meanwhile, the Bible, generally understood to exemplify monotheism, characterizes divine plurality in many passages. Nephilim, or half-gods, appear in Genesis (6.4) and Numbers (13.33). The Lord is pictured in 1 Kings (22.19) on a throne with the host of heaven sitting to his right and left. Psalm 29.1 addresses "sons of gods" in Hebrew, translated in the King James Version as "heavenly beings." Angels appear as manifestations of the Lord and may include him (Genesis 18.2-8, 19.1, and *passim*). References to the Lord's plurality occur as well in the Babel story (Genesis 11), and the book of Job, where Satan, another immortal power, is one of the sons of God. The strongest evidence of non-singular divinity is probably the text's plural form of the Lord's name, *elohim*. A case, then, exists for a less stark distinction between the two faiths than are normally drawn.

Because mythology is difficult in its dealing with the very broad category of belief-systems, it requires some defining of terms, ways of organizing and limiting scope, and, since the subject of beliefs is sensitive, some ground rules.

We inescapably reflect being products of our own cultures—"when you wear leather on your feet, the whole world is covered with leather"—even in what seems today a diverse environment, with rich and seemingly infinite resources of information. Despite nuclear energy and space stations, we absorb, like the least sophisticated societies, numerous unchallenged assumptions. A respectful stance with regard to unfamiliar belief stories can bless us with enlightening perspective on these assumptions. The experience of hearing the creation stories of the Zuni of New Mexico, the Ashanti of Ghana, and the Japanese of Asia can evoke the "ahah!" of discovery. This experience would be akin to strolling along a street in India and observing cows foraging in front yards and impeding busy traffic with impunity, being gloriously decorated on their annual holiday and regularly shooed away by annoyed housewives. The observer suddenly grasps not only that these creatures are regarded as sacred by millions of people, but also that that sacredness is complicated and the world is animated by beliefs entirely mysterious to us.

Something in the human imagination, beyond ordinary curiosity, is touched by this mystery, otherness, the bizarre, the exotic. What people would find unsettling in their everyday lives is safely enjoyable through stories. Narratives that weave together the familiar with the wondrous seem to satisfy a yearning to play with issues of credibility and identity. For example, masks are universally fascinating: "I am not who I appear to be." But the history of the study of mythology, like that of its sisters, anthropology and literature, is tainted with bias reflecting condescension toward the "quaintness" of "primitive" people. The introduction to one collection uses the word "primitive" six times in its first paragraph, when "pre-literate" would have served. Another makes frequent use of the label "savages." Carl Jung uses these words and adds "pre-conscious."

The first books popularizing mythology as a coherent subject sprang from a less enlightened culture than ours in at least this respect: Thomas Bullfinch and Edith Hamilton were part of a colonialist mind-set that perpetuated notions about the inferiority of non-Christian cultures, of people who dressed (dress) and worshiped (worship) differently from themselves. This historical bias in the treatment of different-ness has made for patronizing reactions to discoveries of and about alien cultures that, ironically, advancing technologies facilitate. And, of course, lives have been lost, as when the new medical profession in medieval central Europe tried to eradicate the long-established profession of midwifery. Nature-worshipers of Wicca have been over many centuries either cartoon-trivialized (and still are, hags on broomsticks) or shunned as menaces to soul and society. Part of "civilized" beliefs has long encompassed sexual modesty and an incapacity to comprehend, for example, the Hindu compatibility of eroticism and piety. Edith Hamilton, not seeing a way to modify Ovid's story of Myrrha, a young woman who lusts for her father and goes to his bed, simply left the story out.

Mythology has grown increasingly immediate for me, after academic introductions that placed it seemingly long ago and far away. The long-ago aspect stemmed from my inspiring professor H. D. F. Kitto, at Bristol University, a distinguished scholar before whom I felt imbecilic but had the sense to be awed by his descriptions of the ancient Greek world. So awed that I later lived in Greece for a year to learn the language(s) and sit alone within the Acropolis at a time when that was stunningly possible, communing with Professor Kitto's ancients. But not long ago, in Durban, South Africa, I spoke with women from around the continent who explained that witchcraft is presently a common basis for acquiring the property of an older unmarried woman. By accusing her, members of the community have a chance to seize all of what she owns. Another current practice involves body parts of people born albino. These sell at a high price for medicines, making each day of life hazardous for the thousands born with that pigment deficiency. Anyone who attends the annual Indian Gopastami sees in the decorating of cows inside the temple the contemporary devout enthusiasm. And headscarves, skullcaps, and turbans in any major city tell us that belief stories are very much alive.

The far-away aspect came from another of my inspiring professors, Margaret Mead at Columbia University, who would enthrall the class with stories and films of trance-dancers in distant Indonesian Bali. That exotic aspect, though, was dispelled when one of my brightest students, a Catholic physics major from Missouri who later earned a Ph.D. in linguistics, settled into grown-up life as a North American shaman.

We are all likely to harbor agendas behind our zeal to present and support an enlightened view, and I will declare mine. It has become clear to me over the decades that a sparsity of humaneness is rooted in a failure of imagination.

How *can* someone cut off another person's head? Cold brutality depends on making that other person unlike ourselves. That is why research on the history of hatred shows, as in the Nazi regime, the efficacy of cartoons depicting people who belong to a certain group as sub-human, cockroaches or rats, not-me-or-mine.

When the imagination learns to dehumanize a group, the detachment from the now-alien subject makes cruelty creep by inches from bearable to acceptable to desirable, even to honorable, as one sees in headhunting tribes. An act that would be punished as murder within the group reaps the highest glory if it is done to the outsider. Myths, repeated and repeated, teach members of a society who the insiders and outsiders are, and how to think about them.

An aggressor's distancing himself from a potential victim is necessary, because once it might occur to him that that opponent is actually just like him, his weapon hand might hesitate. Homer, grasping this notion three thousand years ago, shifted back and forth between deadly enemies in their separate camps, honoring the same gods and values, suffering the same griefs, practicing the same rituals. It appears that Homer's wisdom involved love for both sides. Because of this wisdom, and the reliability of available texts compared with, say, Bantu stories, I've chosen to depart from the custom of beginning a study of mythology with the Greeks, and instead work towards them, and culminate with how Homer deals with their beliefs.

Suppose the English poet Percy Bysshe Shelley was even a little bit right. He argued in "A Defense of Poetry" that poets (story-makers) serve the civilizing function of sensitizing us to the fragility of other souls. If that is so, then we would do well to get familiar with the story-making of many cultures. If Shelley was/is correct, we would be less likely to bomb them, starve them, or turn our backs on their gasps for survival.

This breadth of exposure, this cultural journey, poses an ironic problem for serious students. They realize how true for the Aztec, the Inuit, the Navajo, the Egyptian, their holy stories were and are, though these people and their ways may seem strange to us. Seniors in my class were outraged, for example, when the U.S. Supreme Court ruled in 1990 (opinion written by Justice Sandra Day O'Connor) that the U.S. Corps of Engineers could tear up a Native American tribe's sacred burial ground because theirs is not a "true" religion.

Serious students come to understand how ethnic struggles in Europe, Africa, South Asia, and the Middle East are actually often complexly right-versus-right, blind men all tugging at parts of the same elephant, that Sunni and Shiite are more similar than each is to Mormons in Utah or Norwegians. But assigning weight to all religions may leave the student feeling culturally relativistic, frozen in neutrality. It is not easy to live a life like that, especially in raising a family, with offspring pressured by peers and advancing interesting questions. Sophistication does not come cheap.

So they have frequently raised this issue of the risks involved in impartiality. My response always has been this: life will somehow make you have to choose. And when you do, you will be well equipped. Like a physicist or a good judge, a mythologist need not be without his or her own beliefs in order to be open. The trouble with our much-troubled world is in being closed by one's beliefs.

Finally, a personal anecdote. The renowned theologian Paul Tillich held a seminar at Esalen Institute in Big Sur many years ago, and as I lived nearby, I went to hear him. After his key address his admirers were too awed to disturb him and left him sitting alone to rest. I fetched a glass of water and took it to him. With a gentle smile, he thanked me and said, "You are truly a Christian." Well, I was not, and part of me wanted to correct his assumption that kindness was defined by one religion—his. But in the spirit of what I took him to mean by the word, I thanked him, smiled, and nodded.

Although my primary purpose in this book is to make the glorious belief stories and their cultures more manageable, it will delight me if this other accomplishment results, the old-fashioned term "tolerance," which has long struck me as too minimal but now seems like something I'd settle for, as a start.

Chapter One

Functions Myths Serve

WHEN PEOPLE belonging to Western culture think of the word "religion," what generally comes to mind is a benign male divinity—albeit in Christianity one in three manifestations—who sustains a personal relationship with his worshipers. But if religion is to include belief-systems the world over, it needs a broader definition. Most religions, in fact, subscribe to more than one deity, and these are of both genders and sometimes animals—driven by an assortment of moral intentions. They engage in various kinds of relationships among themselves as well as between themselves and mortals. Among the Miwok people of California and Oregon, Coyote is both a trickster and the ancestor of human beings. In a number of Native American tales, animals in council determined our coming into being and our form. For the ancient religion of Hinduism, invariably labeled as polytheist, one supreme immutable power, Brahman, is represented in countless versions and manifestations. The predominance of female deities from pre-history has been coming to light with modern field research and academic resilience. And some ancient belief-systems, like Buddhism and Jainism, do not espouse the notion of a supreme creator-deity. They are closer to philosophies than religions, their worshippers focusing on right behavior.

If one seeks a definition that embraces all religions, that is, all belief-systems, here is one that seems to work. A religion is a community's cherished system of ideas and images connecting eternal and ethical issues, and evoking an attitude of reverence or awe. Without that last part, philosophy might satisfy the definition. Without the community aspect, we would have anyone's personal notion—or poetry.

Dictionary definitions of a cult would, interestingly, apply to the world's major religions. The *American Heritage Dictionary* offers: "A system or community of religious worship and ritual, especially one focusing upon a single deity or spirit." *Webster's New Collegiate* has: "a system of worship of a deity; as the cult of Apollo." Christianity was at first regarded as one of numerous cults of its day. It would appear, then, that social acceptance with wide following distinguishes a religion from a cult. It is hardly surprising that, as with the word "superstition," terms loaded with disapprobation apply to the other fellow's belief. Few people today would be inclined to honor with the name "religion" Jim Jones's set of beliefs which led to his followers' suicide in Jonestown, Guiana, in 1978. With the distinctly negative connotations of the words "heathen" and "pagan," dictionaries relegate to these categories all beliefs other than Old-Testament-grounded Christianity, Judaism, and Islam.

What patterns, then, can we say connect the belief-systems that we distinguish from cults yet are diverse in content and practice? What links together the religions of Hindus, Navajo, Moslems, Sioux, Buddhists, Cree, Christians, ancient Greeks and Hebrews, modern Ibo and Zulu, Alaskan Inuit and Bushmen/San?

Religions or belief-systems are by and large composed of three interrelated aspects: (1) doctrine, or set of precepts, (2) ritual, or rite, and (3) story. The story part is myth, so that we can regard myth as religion en-storied. Each of these three factors, in no hierarchical sequence, reinforces the validity of the other two and contributes to their purpose. Not all three elements, especially ritual, are conspicuously present in material that anthropologists and other researchers have gathered or literature discloses, but are often implied through myth.

Doctrine—or creed, dogma, law, canon, precept—is the body of principles that a society honors, enforces, and teaches, for example, the Ten Commandments in Judaism or the Eight-fold Path in Buddhism. These standards of conduct are the sociological factor in a belief. If a community is to survive as a community it has to do so through order and a binding sense of what is proper. Individuals and the group have to learn to distinguish what is admirable behavior from what is anathema, which killing is murder from which is heroism. Homer often refers to what is "seemly," and in scene after dramatic scene demonstrates the definition of the term.

Doctrine is sometimes not declared but connoted in myth, because the society has completely absorbed its "shoulds" and "should-nots" and applies them in dramatic situations. Whether declared or connoted, doctrine is the glue of social order. The critic Joseph Wood Krutch has said of literature that it always manages to describe the good life. When Homer's characters on the battlefield ponder how to defend a comrade, the reader learns how essential it is to bury the comrade's body, because leaving it as carrion for dogs will doom the man's spirit to wander endlessly without rest. By the same token, Antigone regards herself as obliged by the gods to cover her dead brother's body even with a symbolic sprinkling of earth to ward off this doom, at certain penalty of death, as ordained by King Creon, her uncle. The belief about what happens to the body informs the design of the story, just as the story commits the belief into the group's cultural memory.

A second aspect of religions, then, is story. It would be an unworkable task in most societies to perpetuate beliefs without the vehicle of narrative; it would seem indispensably for the young. For example, a story surrounds the doctrine of the Ten Commandments, telling that Moses delivered the Tablets from Mount Sinai at the culmination of the Israelites' escape from Egyptian bondage and their wandering for four decades in the desert. Whether or not something like this event happened, whether it is legend rather than myth, or even history (Biblical historians estimate the time about 1250 B.C.E.), the engaging, well-wrought story makes the laws more accessible and more memorable. Even in the branch of Mahayana Buddhism called Zen, which subscribes to self-contemplation rather than scripture, guidance on how to live comes through a collection of indispensable exemplary anecdotes. For example, one of the most famous Zen anecdotes is this: after two priests carry a woman across a river, and one later asks whether that contact was inappropriate, the other replies, "I set that woman down hours ago. Are you still carrying her?" The story and the doctrine support each other, the story giving abstractions the vitality and solidity of images, and the doctrine giving the story purpose and scope. The third element, ritual, helps to bind them both.

Ritual is a habitual (traditional) community practice of an activity not biologically required for survival, and intended to achieve effects according to a shared belief. It therefore draws upon doctrine and story. While animals are described as practicing rituals, arguably for security and mating purposes, they are (as far as we know) devoid of doctrine and story. For human beings, rituals can be thrilling and reassuring, as they repeatedly cohere a group.

We tend to recognize religions by their ceremony and pageantry. A series of behaviors is associated with the Easter season for Christians, on Ash Wednesday, during Lent, and on Easter Sunday and Pentecost. The story element is the death and resurrection of Jesus as the Christ, or Messiah, Deliverer, Redeemer, and the doctrine draws from the Gospel (New Testament books of Matthew, Mark, Luke, and John), other parts of the Bible, and particular teachings developed within various sects regarding worshipers' relation to the Christ.

While story gives shape and purpose to rituals and image to doctrine, at the same time rituals like dance and song—hymns and chants—are the powerful means to reinforce both story and doctrine. In connection with the Ten Commandments, observant Jews each year at their Passover dinner, in recalling symbolically an event ascribed to the thirteenth century B.C.E., re-dedicate themselves and teach anew about their covenant with the Lord of the Pentateuch (Torah), the first five books of the Bible. The group's focus is always on the children in attendance, with games, dialogue-roles, and participation in the reading. Rituals such as the serving and partaking of bitter herbs to signify their plight, salt water for their tears, mortar made of apples and nuts for the labor under the Egyptians, unleavened bread to recall the haste of departure, all render as immediate the myth (narrative) of the release from bondage and the doctrine of the Lord's promise to cherish and protect the Israelites. The fact that unleavened bread had been the fare of all dwellers of the region was no more relevant to myth and ritual than the fact that circumcision was a common regional practice (in Egypt, for example), not exclusive to Israelites.

In parts of the world where multiple gods animate the religious atmosphere, some associated with beneficence and others with evil and destruction, the same triad of elements applies. According to the ancient religion of Jainism, followed by a million people in India today, all living creatures, no matter how small or apparently insignificant, are possessed of spirits, so that it is an offense not only to eat them, but also to harm them in any way. Without faith in a supreme god, they subscribe to right behavior, which among the more literal of adherents involves wearing a gauze mask to prevent the inhaling of tiny insects, and carrying a broom to sweep aside small creatures one might step on. Thus their perpetual daily rituals express and reinforce their doctrine of the sanctity of life.

Non-human creatures often have immense powers attributed to them. In Paraguay's Lengua origin story, God in the shape of a beetle created man and woman to be the parents of mankind, and then retired. Some North American tribes maintain the belief that Raven or Grebe (a loon-like diving bird) created us. In others, human beings emerged from deep underground, assisted by animals along the way, our bodies adapting to the (detailed and often ribald) demands of the new environment. Among the Miwok ("the people") tribe, several hundred of whom still live in the San Francisco Bay Area, Coyote plays a role in many variations of creation stories. In one, Coyote, the most cunning of creatures, prevailed over all the other animals at council to create Man as he wished him to be. "After Coyote had completed making the world, he began to think about creating man. He called a council of all the animals" (Van Over, 40).

The Old Testament, on the other hand, has the Lord assigning to the first man, Adam (Hebrew "man," derived from the word for "earth"), complete sovereignty over all creatures of land, sea, and air (Genesis 1.26-28, 2.19), a sovereignty signalized by the power to name them. "So out of the ground the Lord God formed every beast of the field and every bird of the air and brought them to the man to see what he would call them; and whatever the man called every living creature, that was its name" (2.19). All of these narratives carry and reinforce a set of relational attitudes towards other creatures in our world. Those who follow what Westerners call "animism"—ascribing animate and inanimate entities with a soul or spirit, would not think of killing an animal without thanking its spirit, as with the San people in southern Africa.

If myth is the story part of this triad of doctrine, ritual, and story, then obviously myths are not trivial, nor are they errors in thinking, because transcendent experience, at the heart of all faith, is serious, ineffable, and unarguable. What divides peoples who may be touched by or arrive at the same transcendence is form. If the Miwok believes our ancestor was the trickster Coyote, and the Quran/Koran assures Moslems that there is no god but all-powerful Allah, somehow through the various forms, access to a window into divinity is available to all. If contemporary belief-systems from Navajo to Hindu to Christian contain the story element, as they do, then myth is not a matter of defunct collected tales.

One anthologist of world myths who distinguishes between "primitive societies" and "white man's civilization," wrote in his introduction that myths "once [sic] supported the moral order, vitalized secular and religious institutions and stimulated the creative arts in ancient civilizations" (Van Over, 12). Anyone who today stands beneath a balcony in Bhaktapur, Nepal, awaiting with others the daily appearance of the pre-pubescent goddess, knows that not only his own familiar religion is alive.

This book proposes an approach to the vast and rich, though here necessarily incomplete, material of religions' story worlds. The intention is to draw on a sufficient number to support and clarify the central model of three interrelated elements and how they function interrelatedly.

Chapter Two

The Need For Story

IN GREEK, *mythos* means simply "story." For mythologists and ethnologists, people who study cultures around the world, myth is the story aspect of any belief-system. The word, however, has come, like many other words, to have multiple meanings. Irony certainly exists in the fact that the primary current meaning fostered by journalism and advertising is "falsehood," something that invites debunking, as in "myths about calories," "myths about child-rearing," or "myths about the common cold." When we look at belief stories, however, as an integral element of religions, we rescue them from trivializing and come to appreciate their crucial role.

We can say many things about stories, but above all, they are entertaining. The words "Once upon a time . . ." open a magical door. For the listener/reader at any age, they are the way the human imagination connects what we have experienced with what we have not. Stories bring together familiar sensory stimulation, like the catch in the heart when we find ourselves suddenly disoriented—Odysseus lost at sea—and the relief at rediscovering our way home—Odysseus landing at Ithaca.

Stories can navigate our responses at any age, through tension between peril and security, so much so that we often delight in hearing the same pattern of crisis and resolution again and again, from the Grimm brothers to Shakespeare to Maurice Sendak. Whether we encounter through words a giant who crosses a forest in seven steps, a deep pit where a multi-headed monster lurks in the dark, a pair of ardent lovers barred by their families from meeting, or a journey across rough and unknown seas, a story that holds our attention always contains play between what we recognize to be as familiar as our own bed at home, and what is strange and keeps us in wonder or anxiety, like dragons in the bedroom closet. Grounded in the familiar, the unfamiliar inspires questions and accelerated heartbeats. Could there be such giants? Such dangers? Such cruelty? Such disorientation? Could a sister/brother/parent be so evil? How would I deal with this fearfulness, and it with me?

These examples come from Western culture. But in many cultures, stories are episodic. That is, they do not hinge on plot. Coyote conquers Raven and then moves on to another encounter. Listeners are not waiting to learn what Raven does for revenge; he has played his part. Chinese creation lore has the giant Phan-Ku, born from the egg of Chaos, living eighteen-thousand years and growing ten feet each day, then for no particular reason disintegrating into the various natural elements of the earth—no rival, no betrayal, no plot. But there they are. In stories generated in Western culture, however, conflict and causality are pivotal. In E. M. Forster's famous description, narrative happens when the king dies and then the queen dies, while in plot the king dies and then the queen dies of grief.

Whether stories are plot-based or episodic, they beguile. Not only are they a source of pleasure, whatever their mode, they are somehow necessary as well. They serve individuals and groups in ways as fundamental to religious systems as are creeds. Without the narratives about Buddha, Noah, Moses, Coyote, Krishna, Jesus, Mohammed, Anansi the Spider, and Raven, it would be difficult for the esoteric doctrines associated with them to take hold. Children, of course, depend on stories as vehicles to grasp traditional ideas. Yet long after stories introduce religious notions in childhood, they continue to help adults ground their beliefs in concrete images—the empty tomb, the flight from Egypt, the theophany and tablets on Mount Sinai, Prince Arjuna's charioteer who turns out to be Krishna, the beetle's rolling a ball of dung across the desert floor to create the world.

It is not only the metaphysical grasp, however, the set of beliefs, that stories serve. Listeners from one cultural system can be fascinated by stories from another that do not comprise or compete for their own beliefs. The popularity of children's editions of Native American and ancient Greek, African, and Mesopotamian myths keeps generating new editions. There are currently more than twenty versions in print of *The Epic of Gilgamesh*. This appeal comes in part from the novelty and charm of the stories, and how cleverly they are written, but it rests as well in commonality—that element of recognition, the familiar in the unfamiliar.

All persons have in common the experience of earth, sky, and parent-figures. All depend on nourishment, shelter, climate, language, and society. All experience play and routine, and the mysteries of disease and death. The reliance on the role of food and shelter is particularly evident in children's tales, like Beatrix Potter's "Peter Rabbit," and on language in the universal power of blessings and curses.

Another condition that we as humankind share is that our experience of each day and each lifetime holds some degree of random disorder. Along the way, some things are bound to make us afraid. No matter how well people have mastered the skills of managing their worlds, like Julius Caesar, Ozymandius, Lear, and Oedipus, the forces of physical and human nature will be beyond them, and they will, like the rest of us, suffer losses. For the rest of us, something will kill the chickens during the night, the baby will come down with a high fever, the cows will get sick and die off, the tornado will suck our neighbor's house across the river.

Or an amazing harvest will bless us with plenty. Things will fall unaccountably in or out, regardless of deserving. Events will take place arbitrarily and in jarring sequence, with no comprehensible provocation or pattern. Yesterday Abdul's camels stood right there in clear sight. Last night a sandstorm covered them up, and they vanished along with three tents of Abdul's family. How? Why? At midday on Monday everyone in Madagascar saw the sun go black for what seemed a bleak hour, foretelling the end of all existence.

In the face of such baffling events people naturally try to make sense of things, and efforts to provide coherence are informed by what has reportedly made sense in the past. Notions pass down through the stories that nurture and comfort—and resist modification. These comprise cultural context, in some instances for millennia.

The context for belief stories derives from very practical facts of experience and environment. Africans have no stories set in igloos. Inuit have no word for war. Russians have dozens of words for snow. Plausibility arrives through familiarity, not only in physical settings but also through recognizable shapes or designs of stories—their beginnings, complications, and resolutions. In our Madagascar clan subject to a sudden solar eclipse, Grandfather has always told us that if women were allowed at the meeting-house, the sun would go dark, the crops would fail, and we would all die. With Grandmother nodding assent, he tells those assembled around him what happened once upon a time, when the world went black. Women were spat on, drums and pots were banged to chase them (newspaper report, 1965), and astonishingly, the sun grew bright again. Evidently, it is life-endangering for women to enter the meeting-house. Thus a triad of story, ritual, and doctrine succeeds in reflecting both experience (that the eclipse actually happened) and shaping social behavior (that women, Grandma agrees, must be subordinated).

In a society whose stories rest on cause and effect rather than an episodic pattern, any event in life or story will lead both speaker and listener to set about assigning blame to a person or force. One often finds this behavior following the death of a loved one, person or pet, when the bereaved appears to seek ways to find himself or herself accountable: "If only I would have . . . ." In Western mentality it does not just happen that a rock falls on a car. The driver's previous behavior will disclose how he or she earned the smash. A story in Western culture needs a trigger. It does not say that once upon a time a man was driving and a rock hit his car. The end. It would say that once upon a time a man did something bad or foolish, irresponsible, mean, reckless, whatever, and then/therefore a rock hit his car. Or an evildoer used the rock to take revenge on his family. At some point there must have been a precipitating agent or event.

Cause and effect make for coherent order: if I wear an amulet to ward off tigers, the non-existence of tiger attacks proves its effectiveness. The label "superstition" by which people describe another culture's notions sometimes coils around to fit their own truths. The term *post hoc ergo propter hoc* ("after this, therefore because of this") applies to common causal assertions: it will rain because we washed our car today, or left our umbrella home. We may smile at these half-beliefs, but wonder at more serious causal belief of alien cultures: it rains at long last because the tribe's dancers have worked their intricate steps and sung their prayers accurately this time. Who can dispute this conclusion? But in fact, that kind of thinking is very hard to escape in cultures that emphasize causality, blame and reckoning. In Aesop's fables, animals come to have certain appearances as a consequence of certain actions. While these tales are generally amoral, in cultures influenced by the Bible, fortunate and unfortunate events alike are consequences of a process. "And this is why ever since we have had": labor in childbirth, physical toil, or at Babel, diverse languages. Things do not just happen. In this pervasive mind-set they have a moral provenance.

Hindu and Buddhist causality has to do with the consequences of behavior in the system of Karma, from the word for "doing." The belief, put too simply, is that our proper activities advance us through successive reincarnations, the ultimate goal of which is liberation from that cycle, to achievement of perfect blessedness in a state called *moksha* for Hindus and *nirvana* for Buddhists. The practitioner of meditation who arrives through the experience of Om at a holy state of being works to detach from pleasure and pain while living righteously, that is, according to Dharma (Sanskrit for "law"), the rules of personal conduct. In Hinduism, arriving at connectedness of Atman (self) with Brahman (eternal divinity) through meditation, along with righteous conduct, can triumph regardless of the caste one is born into. Not outside forces, not even deities, but personal responsibility governs human fate. These are extremely moral systems.

In Genesis and succeeding books of the Bible, morality is stressed through the close (at first anthropomorphic) presence of the Lord, primarily by the crucial act of creation and subsequently by the covenant he establishes. The text reiterates how the Lord's function as Creator places (Israelite) humankind into a position of obligation/obedience to him, and places himself into the position of provisional redeemer of those he has created. In Hinduism, on the other hand, creation is only a part of divine action, with Brahma, Vishnu, and Shiva as creator, preserver, and dissolver. To be dissolved (destroyed) is only to be consigned to repeat the cycle of subjugation to pleasure and pain, with liberation from that cycle being achievable by personal discipline. Pain, suffering, squalor—all are assumed.

Meanwhile, many myths account for negative experience. The ancient (2000-1200 B.C.E.) Hittite tale of the creator-god Telipinu has him awaking one morning in a dyspeptic mood, putting his left shoe on his right foot and right shoe on his left foot, and leaving home, abandoning human beings, animals, and crops to desolate barrenness. All the earth's animals assembled in council try in vain to coax him to return, but only the humble bee is successful. Without apparent awareness reflected in the text of life-supporting pollination, the story makes the bee responsible for sustained fertility. Why did Telipinu stomp off? Why did earth suffer barrenness for a time? Telipinu's crankiness is a given. Crankiness happens. And unlike science fiction, cultural belief stories always have to end with a picture of life as one finds it, a peopled earth.

In the Homeric Hymn to Demeter, we find the disguised

goddess grieving for her daughter Persephone, abducted by Hades, ruler of the underworld. Visiting Eleusis, the town that the story establishes as the site of her cult, she threatens to destroy the human (Attic) race, so that, for a time, as in the Hittite tale, crops die and animals are barren, a phenomenon probably in some degree familiar to the region from time to time. The resolution arrives, as it must, fostered by a for-once-gentle Zeus, with the plan for his daughter Persephone to dwell one-third of the year in Hades and two-thirds of the year with her earth-nurturing mother, thereby accounting for the changing seasons. The fact that Demeter was already deity of the seasons before this cosmic negotiation has never detracted from its serving as an etiology, a tracing back from observable evidence, in this case from seasons, through story to its origin.

Not only in creation stories, then, the outcome of events is in accord with and therefore supported by nature's proof, as with the salt formations standing where Lot's wife in Genesis (19.26) was transformed. Most conspicuously, however, outcomes in creation tales are visible, incontrovertible. Human beings do in fact exist on earth with certain attributes.

Etiology is a crucial concept in the examination of myths. C. Kerenyi, drawing from Malinowski *(Essays,* 5-6), disputes this fact, but what both are referring to is the service of myth to provide a rational explanation to worshipers, whereas etiology occurs not in "explanation" but in the correspondence of story to experience as an accounting or dramatization of phenomena. For example, in the Hittite toothache myth, which is accompanied by a ritual chant instructing how to pull the tooth, the creature Worm pleads with the god of wisdom, named Ea, for permission to burrow in men's teeth (Kramer, 123). Ea refuses at first, but eventually relents, with some minor penalties, minor from the human point of view. If Ea is wisdom itself, therefore humankind's ally, how could this happen?

Toothache is a fact of human experience. (In the German language one announces having a toothache in words for "it worms me.") The story could not have ended differently and be accepted. Similarly, the conclusion of the Genesis narratives would have to correspond with men's labor for food, women's pain in childbirth, and snakes' being despised and condemned to crawl. Along with banishment from paradise and its concomitant access to the fruit of eternal life, according to the Babel story we suffer as well the dispersal of languages—lest we rival the gods.

And with evil perpetually thriving, Satan, like all destroyer-deities, is never annihilated.

Throughout the continent of Africa, variants of tales have evolved, without surviving rituals, that demonstrate how death came about. Its cause is largely that the creator god (variously named Mawu, Nzombi, Nkengo, Kalumba, Leza, Nyambe, and among the South African Hottentots the Moon), had intentions to offer humankind eternal life, but either didn't care enough or didn't know enough to prevent death.

An example of this pattern that occurs all over the African continent is from the Ashanti people in the Ivory Coast in the West. God sends a goat to inform the seven human beings that they will die but go to live with him in the sky afterwards. While the messenger-goat lingers to forage, God sends a sheep with the same message, but the sheep informs people that their death will be final. When the original messenger, the goat, arrives, people have already accepted the sheep's version and refuse to believe him. What they believe is what will be. The tale mentions that some variations reverse the roles of sheep and goat, but the point of the story is that God is not in control, not to blame for the fact that our lives end. There can naturally be no other outcome than death, but neither the intention of God nor animals, nor the conduct of men, is made accountable. In some variations the intruding messenger is a mischievous bird or animal, who goes unpunished as the creator figuratively shrugs his shoulders.

The creator deity in South Sea Island tales operates by trial and error, as does the Earthmaker of the Sioux-speaking Winnebago tribe in Wisconsin. He discovers his abilities step by step as he proceeds to create the natural world and man as his companion. An example of an imperfect creator, in contrast with the Biblical Lord who is certain of his intentions and able to complete them, is in a story from the Philippines, a matchless example of ethnocentrism. Like many other creators, this one finds himself lonely (inevitably for the story to get going) and decides to fashion some clay into the form of a man. Inexperienced in such matters, when he places it in the oven to bake, he leaves it in too long, so that the man is darker than he wanted, so he places him over in Africa. Starting again with a freshly molded clay man, he overreacts and leaves it/him in the oven too briefly, with a too-pale result, which he places in North America and Europe. At last he learns by the third attempt and gets the desired medium-tan person, whom he keeps in the Philippines. Like all other creation accounts, this one accords with what we have, and goes a step further in its ethnic implications.

Plot stories, with their tension between the forces of danger and security, elicit a response rooted in both a need for order and an attraction to what might be called "theater."

The lure of the dramatic is apparent in daily living,

when, after some great calamity like an earthquake, people are at once shaken by the disruption of order and inclined to flaunt the slightest association with victims. "My brother-in-law's cousin was only two blocks away." People seem ready to lay claim to reports of how they barely missed some dreadful fate.

We are somehow enlivened by disaster, no matter how we fear it, or perhaps in proportion to how much we fear it. Those who are close to death, or have come close to succumbing to it, can possess for others an alien and awesome quality about them, as if they have visited or participated in some other dimension. Consider tales (and jokes) of the magical deathbed statement.

This balance between the yearning for order and the appeal of danger is demonstrated by all familiar children's stories—for example, Potter's tale of Peter Rabbit. On the one hand, Farmer McGregor is a mortal threat, having had Peter's father baked in a pie. Peter's own propensity to restless curiosity, too, is a danger. But these dangers create the excitement of adventure. On the other hand, the reader enjoys Peter's security through Mother Rabbit, with her nurturing grocery basket and predictable good sense, her gentle yet firm management of her family, and the cozy hollow in a tree where the family makes its home. The intrusion of terror into normalcy makes for the drama. Shirley Jackson's classic horror story "The Lottery" begins with assurance of conspicuous ordinariness, through aprons and apple pie.

This tension between peril and security applies in the Homeric epics and the cinema. The solidity of Homer's values, along with the loyalties of particular gods, carries Odysseus home at last to Ithaca. This solidity, however, is in contention with both the hero's own early intemperateness and the hazardous and sometimes phantasmagorical obstacles that keep thwarting him. These are causally related in that Odysseus's early rashness, which he learns to tame, has provoked the powerful deity Poseidon. As with Peter Rabbit, his tendencies portend trouble. Movies—Westerns in particular—depend on both the presence of danger and the likelihood of its being defeated. Audiences would not tolerate a hero who was so weak that his failure was inevitable from the outset or his victory implausible. Neither would they tolerate a hero so strong that his adversaries had no chance to threaten and test him. A too-weak villain leaves audiences bored; a too-strong villain causes distress.

What is in peril does not need to be a farm, an army, a kidnapped child (John Wayne seeking Natalie Wood in "The Searchers"). A marriage may be at risk, or a parent-child relationship, or one's sanity (Ingrid Bergman in "Gaslight"). And the stabilizing order can come not only through the predictable strengths of a Mother Rabbit, the cavalry, John Wayne, or an idealistic congressman; it can spring from a sudden decision, like that of Rick (Humphrey Bogart) in "Casablanca" to sacrifice personal love for patriotism, or in a recognition of one's place in nature. In Shakespeare, stability always comes with the restoration to power of the appropriate governing forces, like King Fortinbras at the conclusion of *Hamlet.* The menace is confronted, and it passes. But in the span of time when it holds sway, we are engaged.

By whatever design the story delivers its crisis-gripped circumstance back to order, it always brings order to the listener as well, by virtue of the story form itself—a shaped, linear, repeatable entity—with structure building towards a conclusion. With the welter of life itself as unsusceptible as it is to management, it is easy to see why people are drawn to the selection, containment and repeatability of events that every story manages. Story lends structure to experience, as do its fellow components of belief-systems, doctrine and ritual.

The particulars of plot vary according to cultural and natural history. The menace of a great flood in the Mesopotamian region, which may have actually occurred, spawned variations of a Great Flood story, most notably and artfully in the Sumerian-Akkadian-Babylonian *Gilgamesh Epic* and the Hebrew Book of Genesis. Only in neighboring Egypt is there no such narrative. No matter how artful the narrator, it would be impossible to sustain belief in a terrifying flood in a country that prays for, and relies for its very survival on, the annual flooding of the Nile.

Stories that entertain appear to offer a satisfying balance between the eerily terrifying and the reassuringly appropriate. And behind that balance or tension is the shape of the telling, an order in itself–the phenomenon of story.

Storytellers, then, have great power. They inevitably draw upon values from their societies' convictions of what is appropriate, and forge them into attractive narratives. For example, a Blackfoot tribe's story tells of the consequences of a girl who falls in love with her brother; Roman Ovid, less moralistic, retells the tale of Myrrha, who falls in love with her father. Adonis is born from their union. Tales may range widely on a moral continuum, from exemplary to casual, but they address intriguing situations. When stories are appealing, and the society embraces them, the values they contain will be reinforced through the particularity of their images.

A striking example of a story so engagingly told that it eclipses doctrine occurs in the Book of Job, in which the Lord explains/boasts to Satan that he is about to test Job by afflicting him "without cause." This announcement in itself is extraordinary, inasmuch as the Bible's Lord is nothing if not just. After Job's dreadful afflictions, his friends, in their effort to console him, seek reasons for his misery and loss in his behavior, or that of his sons. Job knows otherwise: he is innocent. But the orthodox friends are certain that the Lord would not afflict an innocent man, according to Isaiah and other prophets who declare that everything the Lord does is invariably righteous. So they postulate that Job or his sons were about to transgress, and the punishment was preemptive. Wrong. The Lord recompenses Job doubly for engaging in argument with Him and interceding on behalf of the consolers, whom He harshly rejects. This long poem seems boldly heretical but is so exquisitely written that it made its way into the canon for Biblical scholars to justify its inclusion in Scripture.

The many studies of the poem refer to the Job "poet." According to mythologists, however, myth is not authored by an identifiable artist but is the product of a society. When someone sits down to write a "myth," it is some other thing that person will write—perhaps a fable, a poem, a parable, even a short story. But we can imagine that each society profits from certain highly talented individuals—they might be called mythopoets—whose genius for immediacy and delight lifts and broadens their cultures' stories beyond the ethnocentric. For example, individual mythopoets Homer and Hesiod, roughly contemporary, took traditional threads of material about the Olympian gods and, both reverently, crystallized divergent images of them and their relationships. Homer, though, was evidently the more successful in engaging imaginations.

The interest of both was not so much to instruct as to account for a system. Many captivating belief stories have no moral message to deliver. For example, the Arctic region Inuit tale of Sedna accounts for the existence of sea creatures in the world. After her bridegroom, a bird, betrays Sedna, her father comes to the rescue, but jettisons her from the ship and chops off her fingers when she clings to the boat. This is not exemplary fatherly behavior, but the story's intention lies in another direction. The fingers become fish, and her limbs, also severed, become the mammals of the sea. Sedna has not misbehaved in any way to earn her mutilation, but sea creatures are a fact of existence and must have been generated somehow in a manner that relates them to us. (Inuit, like the names of many indigenous peoples, means "the people.")

Myths, then, the story part of belief-systems, are useful in helping people make sense of incomprehensible phenomena. But in cultures that more easily accept random happenings, for instance many African tribes, narratives are nevertheless compelling. The appeal of storytelling seems to be universal. Why?

Stories help us focus through engagement. So many things more and less important are happening all the time, even when we dream, so many sensations bombard us, that we are pleased for the time being to fix our attention and emotional investment on just Tom Sawyer, Kwan Yin, Anansi, or Pooh Bear. Everything else can recede for the duration, even other stories. There is the relief of clarity and pattern.

Storytelling/listening involves looking at and getting involved with one cast of characters in a set of circumstances. Involvement and focus are gratifying; apathy and diffuseness are not. Consider women doing the wash at the river, relating stories or gossip, in many ways the same thing, for pleasure against the tedium. They form bonds of kinship through these stories that may be quite different from those of neighboring clans. Concentrating on one set of events allows the emotions to gather force. Watchers of a horse race or a movie battle can become excited so that although the competitors may have been unfamiliar at the outset, indifference vanishes along with other events and considerations. Life's battles are reduced to one scenario, one contest, and one question of who–or whose team or clan—will win.

Another achievement of story is to lend pattern to events. Once we grow accustomed to these patterns they seem to be facts of nature. For example, in Western culture we are used to a series of three: three bears, three princesses, three little pigs, three tasks, the Trinity. Popular American joke-lore uses a priest, a minister, and a rabbi, or some such triad. But among people in India and Native American tribes the pattern rests on the number four. In these stories a sequence of four comes to be what sounds comfortable, as with the four directions of the wind, the four conversations in the *Mahabharata* between Yama, god of the dead, and Savitri, the devoted wife who talks him into releasing her husband. Four is what storytellers feed back into the traditional cycle and affirm it as pattern.

In Western stories we also come to expect a rising, augmenting action. Native American tales of Coyote picture him doing one thing, then another, then another, in a string of episodes of apparently equal weight, like a string of beads. But in tales that nurture European-American children, the wolf will huff and puff first at (a) straws, then (b) sticks, then (c) bricks. So it is with riddles. Two incorrect guesses will be ventured before the correct jewel-box is opened, as in European folktales and Shakespeare's *Merchant of Venice*. If the storyteller proceeded out of order, even (or especially) a very young listener would be jarred and would know something was wrong. That ascending (a), (b), (c!) is the formula that cultivates our imaginations and that we return to the culture when the time comes for us to tell tales.

Most stories instruct us in one way or another, sometimes by direct moral statement, sometimes by implication, as dramatic testimonials on proper behavior, or sometimes simply by describing for us the way things are or have to be. For example, while many of the Grimm brothers' tales are not particularly educative, some are very much so. In one, a little girl disobeys her mother by visiting the weird Mother Gertrude down the road. The child promptly gets turned into a log and—as an "it"—thrown into the fire by that inhospitable lady. Mother warned her. We are accustomed to fables and parables that make clear what is offensive and even damnable. Few sermons get very far without depending on stories, and most begin with an anecdote. Training for clergy includes storytelling skills.

But not all instruction is explicit, and not all of it deals with taboos. Whatever way the morality turns, we still learn the society's lore—its recipes, its songs, its dress, its diction, its jokes. In the past century, moving pictures have served to pass on images of the culture's assumptions to its next generations. In gangster films attractive stars may portray anti-social figures, who earn sympathy by being hounded by even less likable, often corrupt people, often in uniform. (In early film years industry codes required that criminals be punished, permitting the audience a moral clarity after it had enjoyed identifying with the killer's gumption and glamour.) The moral complexity of modern films leaves no easy reading of circumstances. But viewers do learn traditional behavior.

They learn how to hold a gun and a cigarette. They see various manifestations of etiquette, and learn what is rude. From earlier movies men learned to stand or remove their hats in a woman's presence, behavior that would arouse stares or laughter today. They learned to read a newspaper in the living room after dinner while the wife cleaned up. From recent films they would learn to help out in the kitchen and nursery and even prepare a meal. They have always learned from movies how to dance, kiss, make love, or talk to a future- or ex-spouse.

By that means, by illustrating what other people do, stories bind together members of a group more effectively than through the mere listing of rules. The focus on specific characters concretizes behavior for the imagination to take hold and remember. The result of this cohesion is, among other unifying emotions, clan loyalty—patriotism, with its positive and negative effects. Killing a member of an enemy clan is a heroic act, while doing the same to one of one's own clan is murder. Members know what they belong to and what that belonging means. They learn the definition and boundaries of their circle.

Such bonding and polarizing into members and outsiders helps a community survive. Members of a community need one another for foraging, defending, and supplicating the higher powers. But it also has heinously dehumanizing consequences, evident in stories that ostracize others. The Nazi party in 1930's Germany initiated its campaign against Jews and other groups by circulating cartoons caricaturing them as rats and other loathed creatures. Most jokes have some stereotype object of ridicule: the Pole, Italian, Jew, mother-in-law, hearing-impaired, and so on, without the tellers' or listeners' discomfort at their cruelty. Jokes as narratives reinforce the group's biases/callousness and give approval for them to continue.

Not only do people enjoy hearing stories, they like to invent and/or adapt them, and for many of the same reasons. First of all, stories allow for focusing. Let us suppose, for example, that an accident happened very close to us on the highway this morning. When we arrive at work we are bursting to tell about it. We have been trained by our story-culture to omit the part of the morning's tale about going to the bathroom, brushing our teeth, buying gas, burping twice, scratching our knee, and even having a truck pull too abruptly in front of us. We select what crafts the story of the accident in a way that will keep the listener's attention and build involvement. Along the way we learn to notice that some people tell stories better than others, and we would like to be one of them. We observe their strategies.

Aside from telling what happened, we often have a dramatic point behind the story as well, or let one blossom. We did not just have an accident this morning, but we add that we knew we would, or we did just because we switched freeways at the last moment. Whatever the point is helps us choose what to include and omit. No matter how unconscious the choices, and they most often are, we are all artists when we recount events. That is, unless we are among those who take two and a half hours to describe a two-and-a-half-hour movie.

The most powerful storytelling makes the audience part of the performance. With the best of yarn-spinners, like Mark Twain when he recited ghost stories, the listeners' mouths will drop open, their hearts pounding. This fact tells us that the process of narrating stories serves yet another purpose. The relationship between teller and listener can make the latter feel "as if" the story is happening, and happening to him or her. The central figure or "I" becomes any of us.

To be the "I" of a spectacle is to enter into a theatricalization of ordinary experience. Life becomes drama, and therefore thrilling. We call any moment dramatic when it raises our adrenalin, regardless of whether the circumstances are joyful or catastrophic. Excitement itself is morally neutral. In fact, medical researchers classifying the relative impacts of different traumas list marriage along with widowhood and change of job. Combatants in warfare report that they felt more alive with gunfire and body parts exploding nearby than at any time in their lives. A lovely painting of a cow standing under a tree in the field may be pleasant, but if the artist includes a leopard in the tree, we have a drama waiting. Our readiness as spectators of collapsing bridges and burning buildings shows the seductiveness of peril. Sharks and snipers are to be avoided but fascinating.

The "let's pretend" of drama, in story as on the stage, allows us both to face the danger and not face it. With stories we accept that what is represented as happening is not really happening. The value of its seeming to happen is the excitement, the adrenalin rush, of being tested and terrified by danger. The value of its not really happening is that the danger will have to be over in time for folks to go home and have supper. The shaping into an ordered ritual allows for closure, after our emotional engagement has made us half-forget that security.

The final advantage of "let's pretend" is that a story, unlike real events, can be repeated time and again. The teller can keep tinkering with it until it is crafted just right, and then tell it repeatedly without change, as classical epics were recited.

Once it achieves its satisfying form, its completeness is a way of arresting and mastering time. Whenever teller and listener return to it, its events stand firmly as they were. Odysseus will always pass by the Sirens without submitting to their lovely songs, because his crewmen will always plug his ears with wax. No matter how many times the story re-occurs, the Trojans will never win the war. The Japanese boy who grew from a peach-pit will always be there to save his elderly parents from drowning. Sleeping Beauty will never have Thanksgiving with Snow White's dwarves or Zeus be overthrown by the Titans.

Once the story is committed to the imagination, the storyteller and listener can enjoy the language that weaves the story. As they anticipate key passages, sometimes joining in the recitation, they savor the words as well as the sensations they arouse. Children always show this behavior when they listen to their favorite books. "And that was the house that Jack built."

This repeatability of the story as a complete artifact is another way that storytelling provides security. The world as that story renders it never has to change.

Story, then, offering all these functions to both the individual imagination and the group's sustenance, is predictably an integral component of belief-systems around the world.

Chapter Three
Sources of Myth

"I KNOW that my Redeemer lives . . . . God, whom I shall see on my side." This state of mind and heart, articulated in the Old Testament's Book of Job (19.25-27) and captured for the ages in Georg Friedrich Handel's oratorio "The Messiah," is hardly limited to Judeo-Christian culture. It reflects a universal yearning for an invincible protector and vindicator. Belief stories in their various colorations, plots, and patterns, are grounded in this desire. Not only religions but popular culture as well expresses just this impetus to abate powerlessness. From "My Bodyguard" to "Spiderman" and "Wonder-Woman," and, of course, "Superman," some figure is called upon to rescue a community. The figure needs to be sufficiently like ordinary humankind to comprehend our needs and fears, and at the same time sufficiently superhuman to relieve them. Myth shares so many elements with popular culture that the distinction is easily blurred. But in religion, the group turns to tribal elders and ancestral spirits for more than cures and problem-solving. Strong heroes like Achilles and Samson are admirable agents of comfort, but none so powerful as deities, the benign to be exhorted, the destructive to be placated. Superman may save the day, but neither he nor Clark Kent knows the larger answers.

The search for mighty championing to save the day is expressed in myths worldwide. As distinct from popular culture, myth relates to what is sacred in two respects: first, it addresses the most profound concerns the human heart can frame: Who am I? Where did I come from? Where will my loved ones and I ultimately go? What becomes of us after death? How did the universe with all its beings come to operate as it does?

The second quality that makes myth sacred is that these questions are framed with an attitude of reverence toward a divine power or powers that their worshipers count on to be responsive and responsible. That deities may respond is, of course, the basis of prayer. If they are to be moved by means of intense communication, they must be capable of understanding what is asked of them. And not only when death threatens does the heart turn prayerful. That outreach occurs also in extremes of gratitude and joy. People universally, through whatever institutions and forms they develop to express it, incline toward a notion of the sacred.

The stories that societies shape emerge from a number of sources in human psychology. No one can say for certain what those sources are, and probably no one ever will. We can only put together our best guesses. Here are five:

(1) The fact that we die, and that we are aware that others die, leaving a void. Yet when these others die—whether we love or despise them—they seem also to remain present. That is, we know that something of the person manifests itself with us, something perceivable as the person's spirit or ghost. Though we may be completely certain that these peo-

ple no longer exist, it is just as certain that we can imagine ourselves being with them, even experience conversing with them. While some tribes shape their stories to the idea that the dead carry malice and must therefore be buried at a distance, other tribes live with benign images of their dead kept as close as possible, right beneath their floor. Whether the tone is menacing or benign, the dead are not extinguished.

Myth-poets over the centuries have played with this idea. What is it like, they wonder, to communicate with a spirit? Achilles, the Achaean hero in the *Iliad,* reaches out to embrace the ghost of his slain comrade Patrocles, but his arms pass right through the air, as in the *Odyssey* Odysseus's do when he encounters his mother's ghost. When in the *Inferno* Dante's own character steps into a boat, his weight lowers it in the water. But his companion and guide, the spirit of the poet Virgil, steps in and the boat remains still. In a California Yokuts story collected by Theodora Kroeber, "The Man's Wife," a husband follows his dead wife to the next world and is unable to forsake making love with her.

Tales abound of human visits to the dead, as that of Egyptian Isis and her journey to retrieve Osiris, and of Akkadian/Babylonian Ishtar's threat to release the spirits from the realm of the dead, which utterly terrifies the host of other deities. Those who are no longer among us are powerful. They have the capacity to exact revenge or wreak havoc, or grant benefits.

(2) The fact that we dream baffling dreams that introduce us to wondrous story-elements. The structure and contents of dream-stories can be so stunningly different from our conscious narratives that they open doors to our other, hidden selves. "There is a dream dreaming us," the Kalahari San people say, according to Laurens van der Post, and we confront in dreams a mental life beyond our control.

It can be terrifying or delightful, clearly pertinent or crazily oblique, but it is always a striking story-element.

When a story—or play or film—conveys an experience that recalls dream experience, we respond to it. For example, films may show a protagonist driving a speeding car that hurtles toward an impasse or detour. The odds look impossible, but the driver defies the practical order of things by virtually flying across the barrier, river, or gorge, and surviving. That is a magical mode of dealing with obstacles that occurs in dreams but seldom in life, and is a successfully appealing device in forms of entertainment. It reflects a yearned-for means of redemption.

(3) The fact of our powerlessness in the world. We are indeed vulnerable in the face of human, animal, biological, and cosmic assaults—warring neighbors, wolves, the plague, earthquake, old age and death. The human condition dwarfs us even before we start taking into account villainy, intrigue, and bureaucracy. As a result, we are naturally drawn to associate with a force or forces of strength, prestige, and authority to mitigate the reality of insignificance and vulnerability. For strength we associate also with groups, institutions, teams, and causes that appear to be victorious, who, if they cannot protect us, at least lend us the confidence of connecting with their winning qualities. The most conspicuous example of that tendency is patriotism, manifest in flags and anthems.

(4) The fact that we enjoy play of the imagination. Through various types of representation, or "mimesis," we see how challenges, our own and those of others, engage us. "Once upon a time" something happened, and listeners become alert to the puzzles of time and event. The "let's pretend" question of "What if?' is compelling. What if this person were really an evil dragon, or a talking horse, or a frog

in disguise—we are somehow enchanted by enchantment, and by disguise—see how people love costumes and masks. The world is peopled with spirits and possibilities. When Gilgamesh's friend Enkidu dies, the river, the animals, the path where Enkidu walked, all mourn his death. The story, reflecting the society, projects onto nature feelings that are familiar to it. All societies have invested their imaginations in the surrounding world.

(5) The fact that human beings are capable of immense joy, an ecstasy (*ekstasis:* the state of being outside the body) of gratitude—as when a child's life is saved— too immense to bestow on fellow beings. They need gods to thank.

Chapter Four

The Challenge of Defining, or What to Debunk

IN SEEKING to define, we duplicate the process of most creation stories, in that when we separate this from that, we know more clearly what we are seeing and talking about.

When Aristotle outlined his views on tragedy and comedy in the fourth-century B.C.E. *Poetics,* he used the word *mythos* to mean simply "fable" or "plot," its root being actually "something uttered." Yet anyone who has paid attention to the word knows that it has come to suggest many things, from dragons and witches, to notions of white supremacy, to cures for hiccups. Like "love" and "truth," it is elastic in its definitions. But one can apply multiple meanings without confusion, as in "I love my children" and "I love hot dogs." It should not be difficult to clarify our uses in their formal and informal contexts.

We read: "Myths about Children's Shoes," "Myths about Cold Remedies," "Myths about Investing in the Stock Market." Advertising and journalism use the word to identify false claims that need to be exposed and punctured. Debunkers of notions about Vitamin C and welfare programs use the word to indicate what some people have the poor judgment to believe, and what people who are informed will want to correct. One would not want to be caught believing a myth. This definition as falsehood is legitimate in that it represents a widespread use.

Another pejorative use of the word "myth" is past-based, indicating that a tale is no longer viable. It refers to beliefs that some primitive people once upon a time held about gods and goddesses. In some cases the past tense is valid. For example, the Aztecs in pre-Columbian times in Central Mexico believed that one day the sun-god would return. This belief led to their fatal embracing of white European invaders, and no longer holds credence with anyone. But myths are often taught in schools with the sweeping use of past tense, as in "the Navajo believed." Most of the Navajo people of New Mexico, however, whose religion is tightly bound to their geographical location, still believe as their ancestors did, speaking their language and keeping alive their nurturing culture, with its complicated creation stories, its Sweat House purification rites, and its highly regulated healing treatment of sand-painting. In World War II, the Navajo language served the U.S. military to foil national enemies. Likewise, Hindus in India, Pakistan, Southeast Asia and elsewhere, Persians in Iran and Afghanistan, and Jews around the world still subscribe to the stories of their ancestors. And the Dalai Lama is presently the anointed fourteenth high priest of the Lamaist religion, which is practiced in Tibet and Mongolia, and among Tibetan exiles in Nepal and India.

The meaning perpetuated by mythologists themselves for generations, like Thomas Bullfinch and Edith Hamilton, who were clearly charmed by Greek and Roman tales, conveyed the quaintness of the tales with condescension while eviscerating them of their sacred content. Thus the ten-year battle for Troy and its aftermath became popularized through the lens of Western cultural chauvinism, offering no threat to contemporary received notions of sacredness. A reader might ask, as students often do, "Who could have believed in gods who behave in such irresponsible ways?"

Mythologists have been trying in the past century to arrive at a meaning for the word that supports an objective study of exotic beliefs, with the goal of taking seriously the stories they encounter from cultures around the world. Joseph Campbell did much in his writings, films, interviews, and classes to popularize myths with respect for their sacred content. Anthropologist Margaret Mead, who was professor as well as curator of ethnology at the American Museum of Natural History, filmed and lectured on the trance-dances of Bali with a scientific eye more than condescension. The idea that is slowly becoming more acceptable among collectors, researchers, and educators is that to point out the commonalities of the many belief-systems is not to diminish the status of the predominant one, but to be open and respectful to all of them.

Because myth shares some qualities with a number of other terms, like fairy tale, people often use them interchangeably. But clearer thinking results from honing to crisper delineations, and so it is useful to play "not-this-but-that" in discussing these terms. It is always the case that using the terms sloppily impedes precise communication. If pie, cake, torte, cookie, bonbon, confection, sweet, dessert, crisp, and cobbler are used as if they all mean the same thing, the image sent to our brain and palate may not match up with what we expect to enjoy.

For that reason, what follows is a set of distinctions,

including differences between myth and folktales/fairy tales, fables, folklore, legends, magic, and mythological literature, and myth's relation to science and history.

The word "mythology" designates either the study of myths or a collection of them.

Like myths, folktales and fairy tales are traditional stories that deal with the supernatural and are ahistorical or atemporal ("a" being the Greek prefix for "without," as in "amoral). This means that the time when they happened is not of interest. Who would ask what year Sleeping Beauty was awakened by a kiss from the prince? They are also alocational, because the forest or castle where events take place in tales is generic—we don't think of looking them up on a map.

Because these tales deal with fairies and giants and such impossible powers as the granting of invisibility, or feats like crossing seven leagues in a single step, people often regard them as myths. A Hindu folktale describes a beetle who strikes a bargain guaranteeing to take only three steps across a designated space, but when the deal is sealed, he proceeds to expand so massively that three steps for him will cross the universe. What we might say separates fairy or folktales like this from myth is the treating of teleological matters (dealing with ends of things), the largest issues we face, issues like how we came to be and where we go after death. Even when they have a moral, like that in King Thrushbeard, in which a haughty princess learns humbleness, eternal questions are not addressed. "Where have my loved ones gone? Who or what controls what happens to my people and me?" In myth these questions are either addressed or suggested.

The most direct way of addressing "Who am I?" and "Where did I come from?" is through the cosmogony (world's birth) aspect of cosmology, which describes the universe as a system ("logos" meaning study, as in psychology or numerology). All belief-systems convey a particular cosmology, or set of images of how the world or universe operates, for example, the sun's chariot traveling from east to west. The term "cosmos" means not just world or universe but world or universe that is orderly, all parts separated and in their places, as opposed to a state of chaos. For ancient Greeks, chaos *(Kaos)* did not mean things in utter disarray but pre-order, a terrifying condition of dark emptiness. The elaborate stories of the Yurok people of northern California and Oregon refer to a beginning in disorder so alarming that their annual earth-pounding dance ritual ensures for them that the earth will remain in balance. The ABC of mythology is Anything But Chaos.

"Cosmogony" means the birth of the cosmos—"gony" deriving from the same root as "genesis," or "coming into being." Mesopotamian, Hebrew, and Hindu mythologies place an emphasis on the creation of the universe. Other systems, for example Native American, put their emphasis on the creation of humankind. Many, particularly Native American and African, emphasize the creation of the animals, the natural world, and the forces of water and wind. Among the San people of what is now Botswana, we learn from their stories, the rolling of a dung-beetle's ball of humble material accounts for the existence of the earth. For the Greeks there seems to have been little interest in the business of creation, aside from Hesiod, in the eighth century B.C.E., who wrote the *Theogony* (birth of the gods), which is mostly a genealogy and chronicle of violent successions, with no attention to the creation of humankind. Hesiod casually refers to Earth's having created Heaven. In more popular works, including the Homeric epics, the Greeks focused on the operation of the universe once it was here, and its impact on human lives. For the Hebrews, everything that follows the Creation in Genesis is linked to that momentous event, through the relationship of the Creator to the created. The covenant that the Lord establishes between himself and various patriarchs remains a perpetual reminder of human indebtedness.

Folklore, often confused with myth, also a body of knowledge that a society passes down through generations, is a broad category that includes secular riddles, recipes, and games. Folktales are part of lore, that body of inherited material, but folklore can also encompass such skills and artifacts as baskets and pottery that follow and perpetuate certain patterns. Sometimes these designs will refer to or derive from the religion, as with Greek god-and-hero-adorned vases and jars (amphora). But folklore is not itself myth.

Fables are fictions, often expressing a cautionary theme and often using anthropomorphic animals as characters, which share with myth their ahistorical and atemporal qualities. No one wonders where and when Aesop's animals carry on their mischief or acquire their spots, stripes, and trunks. But fables use magical exaggeration to invite the willing suspension of disbelief, while myths presume and reinforce belief.

Legend, too, has myth-like qualities, in being a popular narrative passed down through generations, but it springs from historical or presumably historical events, as in stories about Abraham Lincoln, King Arthur, and King Charlemagne. A legend is almost never verifiable but always romanticized.

Magic is a wide-ranging term that applies basically to seeming manipulations of physical nature. This means that it can include sleight of hand, mind-reading, and other apparently supernatural feats that have nothing to do with religion. But as a part of belief stories magic can produce wonderment through transformation, spells, and the like. Although it often serves these narratives, it cannot replace them, as with the burning bush that Moses confronts, the parting of the Red Sea, or the feeding of four thousand people with seven loaves and a few fish (Mark 8).

Because a myth is an anonymous communal story, a type of group sacred poem, what an individual person composes does not conform to the definition. A myth emerges over time from the society, no doubt with strong contributions by its most gifted poets and perhaps its shamans. When the poet becomes identifiable and takes liberties in shaping the traditional material, as with Homer, Virgil, or Ovid, we are really talking about mythological literature. While Ovid portrays the deities with ridicule rather than reverence, and Homer evidently believes in the Olympians, both have woven the inherited stories into works of their own. The same may apply to the Sumerian/Babylonian *Epic of Gilgamesh*, though we lack the poet's name. It is safe to conclude that in the passing on of Inuit and Ashanti tales, the most adept storytellers among the group must have put their stamp on the material.

There are illuminating ways in which myth is related to and sometimes confused with history and science. Both myth and (modern) history describe events that the society supposes once to have happened, for example, a certain eclipse of the sun. But the work of the historian is to discover and verify the actual time and place and the actual context and sequence, whereas for the myth-believer time has dissolved, expanded, or compressed between the original event and the conducting of rituals that re-create it.

In important ways, the event in myth keeps happening

every time the story is revived in the telling, as we see in the Passover ceremony or the taking of consecrated bread and wine in the Eucharist or Holy Communion. The historian's view of an event understands it to be past, finished, in a sense dead, having been replaced by many subsequent events. With each revisit, it may change according to the accretion of information and the test of accuracy, but it is over. The mythical view of an event is that it is present, timeless, irreplaceable, like the Crucifixion, Mohammed's inspiration to write down the Quran/Koran, and Buddha's enlightenment under the Bodhi tree. The great mythologist Mircea Eliade refers often in his writings to the "myth of the eternal return."

Science, too, manifests correspondences with myth. Both describe models of the way the universe operates, including the relation of the planets and the role of forces of nature. In both science and myth, cosmology includes cosmogony, perhaps the Big Bang, originating in a violent eruption, perhaps a peaceful separation of earth and sky into parts by a half-interested creator-deity or a mischievous woman.

Both science and myth make use of models, word-pictures that represent an idea, scheme or notion. Scientific models of the world at one time showed it flat, or at the center of the planets with the sun revolving around it, as in Ptolemy's conception. But these idea-pictures were replaced because of an essential difference between myth and science.

The scientific cast of mind—even its job—is to question and test its own assumptions, to try to progress beyond received ideas about things and processes. The myth-believing cast of mind, on the other hand, is absolutely and literally conservative. In fact, serious danger is perceived in the prospect of disturbing the received idea. The purpose of the story is to reassure the group that what they believe is still unerringly and reliably true.

The definition that serves this book can be expressed both simply and elaborately. Simply put, myth is the story part of a belief-system.

More elaborately, myths are anonymous narratives subscribed to by a community, which convey its most profound questions and most cherished truths. They dramatize a culture's living beliefs, as in a Navajo tale of how the world was created, a Hindu tale of a woman's rescuing her husband from the god of death, or the tale of Moses striving with the Egyptian Pharaoh. Each of these stories has been for some time viable within a culture and associated with rituals and doctrine. By and large, mythologists today are in the process of granting myth that viability long withheld from it.

An understanding of myth begins not in the past but the present. Like science, it gives great weight to physical evidence. Myths about the first people and details about their appearance, myths about toothache, or about dealing with an eclipse, correlate with visible proof. The god of wisdom could not have denied the worm access to humans' teeth, or the story would not have endured over time. We have the evidence. To survive from generation to generation, a story must be credible. When in southwest Native American tribes a baby is named by emerging at the moment an elder calls its name from a list, there is no question of its credibility. The baby heard its name and appeared.

Unsophisticated societies may not know or have known that the universe is probably ten to twenty billion years old, or that we are part of a galaxy among millions of galaxies of hundreds of millions of stars. They observed and observe, however, that it is wondrously vast and yet they themselves are somehow part of it. Human imagination claims that there has to be some connection between that vastness and the way we live out our daily lives. Why do we care how the world began? What do its beginnings have to do with us? These questions can be addressed to the myth-believer and the physicist alike.

Myth-believers and physicists are model-makers. They project pictures to make abstractions palpable and accessible. One astrophysicist, at Princeton, J. Richard Gott, has referred to our universe as "just one bubble in the foam of space-time" (*Newsweek* 6/13/88, 62). The word-picture gives us quick access to the idea, as does the sun-chariot of Phoebus Apollo traveling unfailingly from east to west across the sky. But the second is an unquestionable image, in that the sun (the earth) never changes course. Anyone can observe the evidence.

Here is a picture: the universe starts out by exploding out of nothingness, the size of a dust-grain, and inflates and inflates, dividing into separate entities in a fraction of a second in unimaginable heat. It takes half a billion years for simple atoms to form, five billion more for galaxies, and ten billion for our solar system.

This portrayal has much in common with myth. It describes a process that accounts for the coming into being of the universe that we know. It addresses ultimate questions, so that its narrative supports the accuracy of its cosmology as doctrine. Its authorship is multiple—it springs from a community whose goal is truth even more than beauty. And it is viable. But it is not settled, closed, as a belief would be. It is hypothetical, under scrutiny, on probation, and today scientists are still exploring the question of what preceded the "big bang."

The absence of a personal god or gods is not what distinguishes the scientific model from myth, because there are belief-systems, for instance Jainism, that do not attach personality to the divine. What distinguishes the two is that the scientific proposition exists to be proved wrong. The goal of its subscribers is to challenge and replace it, to expose the weaknesses of their own cherished model. In that way, the modern scientific attitude is radical, whereas there is nothing so conservative as myth. The world no longer accepts Ptolemy's model of the earth at the center of the universe. If Einstein's fundamental contribution must meet the fate of those of Euclid and Copernicus, so be it. But followers of the Buddha, Allah through Mohammed, Jesus as Christ, Krishna, and the Winnebago Earthmaker seek always to preserve and reinforce. Their attitude is that the system is complete.

Myths are always viable within a society because the evidence of their truth is demonstrable in the present. If it were not, a myth would not endure as tradition. Every time we see a rainbow, for example, we see proof of the Lord's covenant with Noah and all living creatures (Genesis 8-17). To the earlier Sumerians (3,000 B.C.E.) and roughly contemporary Babylonians (2000-1000 B.C.E.), the same evidence would signify the necklace that Ishtar, goddess of love and war, displayed in an effort to placate other gods after the great flood. In the Hittite toothache myth the nasty worm receives permission from the god Ea to gnaw in human teeth. Ea, who, being wisdom, is normally friendly to humankind, behaves peculiarly in this situation. But could he refuse the worm's request and banish toothache from human experience? With that conclusion, the myth would not have been perpetuated, because it would not correspond to the human condition.

Myths either describe or imply etiology—the tracing

back to its cause of something presently observable. Sedna, in the Inuit myth from the Arctic Circle region, has her fingers and hands chopped off by her father when they are fleeing in a boat after he has rescued her from her destructive bird-husband. The father's behavior is puzzling—he had been devoted enough to save her—but what is not puzzling is the origin of sea-creatures. We "know" where fish, seals, whales, and the like first came from, and they have a kinship with us, human beings, Sedna being a partly mortal woman. As for human behavior as manifested in the father, it is always mysterious.

The essential work of myths within a group is to preserve its unity or self-identity ("I am of the people of the Winnebago tribe who were created by Earthmaker"), its equanimity ("there is an order to things"), its prestige ("my heroes, my ancestors, and my history are splendid"), and its renewed comfort through purposeful rituals. These rituals, by means of shape, color, taste, smell, and sound—bells, drums, flutes—as mnemonic devices, convey its doctrines. The doctrines instruct how people's behavior relates to the cosmos. The recitation of rubrics, "thou-shalt-nots," without a story context would not take hold as readily. What serves to reinforce notions for the adult community also serves to transmit them from generation to generation as an irreplaceable vehicle for teaching the group's youngest members.

Myths, then, either are or have been viable and etiological—that means they make sense. Yet trivialization and literal emphasis on unfamiliar content have denied them credibility. Although they all serve the same purposes, they express themselves in different forms relative to their cultural settings and values, and these forms collide. How can Moslems, Jews, Christians find any sense in a creation story in which humankind is put together by a coyote (Miwok), who assigns to human beings his own best qualities as opposed to those of other animals in council? How can we accept a picture of animals as our creators? Didn't the Lord give Adam sovereignty over all the animals? Aside from the unfamiliar portrait of authority—a coyote!—with no recognizable deity speaking, members of dominant monotheistic cultures find such creation narratives frivolously amoral at best, blasphemous nonsense at worst.

A creator who is puzzled, for example, a motif common in Native American myth, may be a frightening characterization to those who draw comfort from the authority of a paternal omniscient figure. The emphasis of many sacred tales, however, is not on exemplifying moral values but on describing the operation of a cosmic system that includes the role of nature and other forces of energy. How can sacred be separated from ethical? While this is a jarring notion for many whom the Bible reassures of the synthesis of the two, it is a natural distinction in some cultures. For example, in Hinduism, the same deities often have benign and destructive aspects. The implication is that men, not deities, have to learn how to conduct their lives.

It is far more daunting to provide a theodicy (justification of the ways of God to man) in a framework featuring a completely benign deity who allows evil than in the Hindu plurality of deity-manifestations, each with his or her various aspects and sub-aspects. As modern societies have opened up more to multiple beliefs, expanding to include new citizens with non-Western religions, they are less likely to view belief-systems other than the Judeo-Christian as quaint, exotic, and trivial.

Serious scholars like Bullfinch and Hamilton, locked into a closed culture, would describe Greek and Roman deities as colorful and energetic, but hardly anything a person could plausibly worship. With Western worship founded on a relationship with a single, all-powerful deity, it is inconceivable that a tearful mother with a sickly, feverish infant would carry it to a shrine to Aphrodite or Hermes, silly personalities caught up in minor politics. In the *Iliad*, Homer shows Aphrodite (comparable to Roman Venus) running tearfully to her mother Dione when her hand is injured in battle. Her deity/godhood is defined by her deathlessness, not by her character. "Immortal" means simply "not mortal," not necessarily omniscient, omnipotent, and benign. The tearful mother of the infant would have taken her child for blessing and healing to a shrine of local earth-spirits. And today perhaps we can afford to believe that her prayer, along with those of a Canaanite or an Apache mother, was as devout as any mother's.

To the public at large, we have noticed, myth often means falsehood or misconception, or wrong belief. Between this extreme and the working definition of mythologists, the story that conveys and perpetuates a culture's deepest truths, there are other major uses of the word, neither true nor false. One of these is mythological literature and art. That is the aesthetic and secularized appropriation of myth by identifiable artists such as Ovid's in his *Metamorphoses*, Shelley's in *Prometheus Unbound*, and Botticelli and Rubens in their paintings of Olympians. The apparent secularization in this definition is not entirely accurate, however. It is mitigated by the phenomenon of inspiration, by which the artist, touched by whatever functions as muse, gains access to the very stuff that generates myth. There are many variations on literary use of myth. In Herman Melville's *Moby Dick* the author depicts Father Mapple's revision of the Jonah story from the Old Testament. In his important sermon in the whaling village he omits the final chapter, ironically transforming the meaning into a moral lesson.

Psychiatry, psychoanalysis, and psychology have appropriated the imagery of mythology as a healing tool, largely through the work of Carl Jung, with his influential idea of a "collective unconscious." But not all borrowing has been benign. An example of distorting appropriation of sacred stories is the Ku Klux Klan's notion that Noah's contemporaries were all extinguished for having mixed the races. This use of myth, which we can call institutional, still involves an active belief. On a radio broadcast (KQED-FM, San Francisco, 1972), a spokesman for vegetarianism explained that Homer had been an early proponent of the vegetarian way of life. The speaker found his evidence in the peaceful nature of the Lotus Eaters in the *Odyssey*. But in truth Homer, who regarded ideal citizenry as vigorous social exchange, viewed the Lotophagi as dangerously antisocial, and Odysseus rebukes and chains the men who have submitted to their seductive lotus. In Homer's epics the heroes eat meat whenever they can.

Still another use of the term "myth" is a professional one, in which scholars from diverse specialized fields elaborate on their generalized hunches about "savages" or "primitive man." For example, philosopher Alfred North Whitehead, in *Religion in the Making*, describes a linear sequence of categories through which "man" progressed: from ritual to emotion, which "waits upon ritual," to belief, and finally to rationalization. He expresses pleasure at the adventure of each transition as it fits his model of advancement (21), overlooking the fact that these stages, for example emotion and belief, are likely to coexist.

Marshall McLuhan displays the breadth of meaning that the word "myth" enjoys. He refers to "the mythmaking power of a medium [the movies] that is itself a myth form . . ." (Murray, 296). Comparing myth to advertising, he regards it as "a kind of explanation or mode of intelligibility" (290). McLuhan here joins company with the many teachers of courses in mythology who define myth as "explanation," thereby eviscerating it of its sacred aspect.

The following passage shows McLuhan's understanding of mythopoesis: "It was Newton's *Opticks* that taught poets the correspondence between the inner and outer worlds, between the structure of seeing and the structure of the scene. This notion planted in poets the ambition to gain control over the inner life by a calculus of landscape composition" (Murray, 298). The implication here is that the Bible authors, Plato, Spenser, Shakespeare, Cervantes, and Donne, all of whom wrote before Newton, needed to be acquainted with his work before being capable of creating allegory. This attribution of cerebration in the function of myth is directly at odds with the word's meaning for the anthropologist Bronislaw Malinowski, who deplored pronouncements by theorists who have never lived "in the bush." His position was that "myth, in fact, is not an idle rhapsody, not an aimless outpouring of vain imaginings, but a hard-working, extremely important cultural force" (97).

Probably the most confounding sort of definition of myth is one born of a healthy disaffection with Western intellectuality, but in which words are left to mean anything, with the implication that vagueness is the appropriate response to rigidity. In *Myth and Ritual in Christianity* Alan Watts defines myth "as a complex of stories—some no doubt fact, and some fantasy—which, for various reasons, human beings regard as demonstrations of the inner meaning of the universe and of human life" (7). One may wonder which stories are "fact." Does Watts mean legend? People who read accounts of actual persons, Abraham Lincoln, for instance, know how elusive historical authenticity is. And what does Watts mean by "fantasy"? Further, it is doubtful that believers in a myth "regard" it as demonstration of inner meaning. The distance from experience evoked in the notion of regarding, and the preoccupation with "meaningfulness" are not universal. The wish to feel safe and hopeful in the midst of danger is universal.

The literary critic Mark Schorer has reasoned that myth, unlike the specific experience of mysticism, must be defined broadly and loosely because of the broad nature of its phenomenon. But it is apparent, that while "apple" may be more specifically defined than the broad-natured "idea," the latter term begins to acquire its refinement through distinction from "concept," "inspiration," "thought," "notion," "ideation," and so on. It is the broadest definitions that are the most useless, like the French poet Paul Valery's half-truth, "myth's the name for everything that exists, or subsists, only to the extent that speech is its cause" (Levin, in Murray, 102). Among numerous other instances of nebulous uses is Henry Nash Smith's "a popularly accepted cluster of images" (Dorson in Murray, 84, ref. to *The American West as Symbol and Myth*). A strong case clearly exists for the value of defining such a crucial word as "myth."

Chapter Five

Model Making

A MODEL is a structure or pattern that represents an idea. For instance, a globe is a model of the earth. A blueprint is a model for a house. Stories provide models that provide some order to the random universe of experience. The impulse to storytelling as a way to arrive at this order tends to involve enumerating categories. For example, the Hindu caste system delineates four possible levels of class.

We sort people, objects, phenomena, and time-periods into categories. Institutions like schools and factories could not function for a day without them. Models almost appear as rituals in themselves, as they help maneuver a society from Tuesday to Wednesday. Examples abound, but the educational system is as useful a setting as any for illustration.

Schools and universities divide subjects into disciplines, such as arts and sciences, course programs into bachelor's and master's, departments such as chemistry and French. Although the content and labels of these categories change, as geography and history have largely coalesced into social studies, the existence of categories does not. We cannot manage without them.

Within subject areas we keep subdividing: genus, species, variety; history divides into European, Asian, American—North, Central and South, or foreign and domestic; biology falls into zoology and botany, with their sub-classifications. We travel first, business, or economy class, and are ranked in the military from general to private. For convenience we also divide time into periods. We have daylight savings, though Russia and India excuse themselves from these divisions and maintain one time across several zones. History and literature studies cover the 18th, 19th, or 20th century, or the American Novel from 1914 to 1945, or the Romantic Movement from 1800, or the Medieval Age, all with arbitrary beginning and ending dates, as if on the first day of a century some landmark change took place.

This is all to make processes manageable, like traffic lights and signs. Class periods or modules of one hour, two hours, or an hour and ten minutes make for a conveniently predictable regimen. Everyone involved knows what is required to complete a course of study and where to be and when.

Groupings of food—proteins, fats, carbohydrates—and sub-grouping are ubiquitous. We make clumsy efforts at lumping people into social strata: lower, middle, upper classes, then, not quite satisfied, into upper-middle and lower-middle, then we add the under-class and the top one percent, resorting to income figures for varying definitions. All these help make discourse possible, if not always accurate or productive. Useful discussion depends on some principles of ordering to get ideas across. "By socialism I don't mean X, I don't mean Y, I mean Z." The clearer the speaker, the finer the distinctions to help others follow.

This need for ordering by means of distinctions applies as well in traditional concepts regarding human origin and destiny. The people of many African and Native American tribes tell tales about how the earth was separated from the sky, separation being a means of defining order. The Old Testament Lord also begins by purposefully sorting out the elements of creation from a dark and watery primordial chaos. And perhaps among categories the ultimate distinction lies in the duality of good and evil.

The twelve Olympian deities possess particular roles and duties, as do the three Fates—all these yielding to the force Ananke, meaning "what had to have happened." In the *Iliad* when Zeus has to decide which side will gain victory that day in battle, Troy or Achaea (Greece), he goes up to Mount Ida to consult the three Fates, Clotho, Lachesis, and Atropos, who are believed to control human destiny. The Fates, however, do not themselves make a decision but refer Zeus to Ananke. As in many other belief stories, either stated, as in the Japanese and the Norse, or implied, there are beyonds before beyonds.

Just the use of numbers serves ordering. From the Navajo people's four winds and four directions to the Chinese twelve auspicious signs/animals, to Dante's Nine Circles of the Inferno, numbers suggest control of certainty. And no area of thought is more inclined to seek certainty than the spiritual. Questions compel us.

Where does the soul go after death? Hamlet contemplates two alternatives and concludes that survival with the "slings and arrows of outrageous fortune" is preferable to unknown horrors after suicide, an act that religious tradition has told him is evil. These most profound questions—origins, destinies, and the mystery of evil—offer the imagination rich material, not just for poetic satisfaction, but for survival.

Models vary from culture to culture in describing answers, but models always exist. Hindu tales are so elaborate, with extensive pantheons and creations beyond creations, with the god of death being female in some stories and male in others, that they are daunting to Western peoples as a serious body of material for study and adoption. But over many centuries the vivid stories accounting for an elephant-headed god, Ganesh, son of Shiva, and Hanouman, the monkey god, have been so richly textured that they continue to satisfy many millions.

All myths that succeed in perpetuation after long testing amount to closed systems. When a tribal healer cannot revive an ill patient, it is not for failure of influence with the spirits but some more powerful countervailing influence. And so the healer retains credibility for further patients. So it is with the long-tested system of astrology, and with the religions around us.

When a system offers a weak correspondence with experience, it modifies. For example, the Old Testament depicts a condition of afterlife called Sheol, prominent in the Psalms, as morally neutral, a place to which all souls depart, regardless of their conduct during life. But the Hebrew belief-system, so firmly grounded in morality, was susceptible to influence from the Zoroastrians in Persia, who were steeped in a concept of continuous battle between the god of light, Ahura Mazda, and Angra Mainyu, arch-demon of many disguises, who lures people to lie and deceive. For Persians, and then the Hebrews, if all people arrive after death at the same fate, why should one be good? Does not the Lord stress justice? As the Bible stories eventually move through Old to New Testament, Sheol, the repository of all souls, complicates into categories of heaven and hell, or, for Catholics, heaven, purgatory, and hell. Thus the model as it adapted provides secure and acceptable guidelines concerning the consequences of behavior.

This Lord of justice, who begins in Genesis as a figure so anthropomorphic as to receive pleasure from inhaling delectable smells, and who shuts Noah into the ark (7.16), evolves to a broader, more ineffable and less concrete force, but remains consistently a Creator. Many origin myths portray creators with varying degrees of omniscience. The Winnebago people's single creator-god called Earthmaker, who is more omnipotent than he realizes because he is not omniscient, yearns for someone to converse with; he discovers his power to form a man from clay to be his companion, gifting him with breath and speech.

Not all belief stories have a creator "on high." There are also elaborate emergence myths, prominent among Southwest Native American peoples, depicting the original people's struggle upward from deep within the earth. They acquire physical features as they become needed, for example, eyes for a world with light, as one can now prove merely by observing. Some members return briefly to get their pots and pans, as people might. Tellers of these stories can point out a facsimile of the emergence-point on earth, but the actual place is too sacred to risk violation.

In the very complex Hindu models, the power of gods is mitigated by challenges from both demons and mortals, presenting no end of trouble, with gods transforming to mortals and mortals to gods. This imagery makes the vicissitudes of experience comprehensible and emotionally manageable. In daily ritual offerings in Bali, for example, palm leaves are woven into trays to support elaborate fruit, vegetable, and floral arrangements as offerings for benign deities in the temples. At the same time, simpler and smaller arrangements are placed on the ground to propitiate malign deities—it would be hazardous to neglect these. (Dogs and monkeys make sure they disappear.) The gods exist less to save us, the model shows, than to engage with us.

Another model that places limitation on divine powers occurs in the tales from all over Africa in which the creator decides to send mortals the crucial message that they will not die. But an irresponsible or delayed messenger, in a variety of animal forms, manages to spoil the message. Too bad. The revised message that men will have to die is binding, not because of either messenger's sinfulness or malice, but because things do have a way of getting bungled. And more essentially, because we die.

Categorical models serve not only in the myths themselves, but in the approach to studying them that is the discipline of mythology. For this book, the design to render order to myths is a trio of interrelated circles within the circle of belief-systems. There are other useful models, but it would be virtually impossible to discuss myths coherently without any model at all.

Chapter Six

"Myths" about Myths

A PAIR of giants has stood guard before the gate to appreciating myth's functions. The more obvious barrier is religious conservatism, and the other is the set of limited methodologies better suited to more technical disciplines.

Ironically, the only way that classical myths could survive through the prevalence of both Christianity and scientism has been for them to be emptied of their religious potency and regarded as cultural gems (Eliade, *Myth and Reality*, 157). The work of Edith Hamilton culminates this devitalization.

Through Hamilton's best-selling books, chiefly her *Mythology*, millions of high-school, college, and general readers, while being exposed to her enthusiasm for the Greek nation and culture, have been granted access to the naughty antics of Zeus/Jove, the marital squabbles between him and Hera/Juno, the vanity of Aphrodite/Venus, the ill temper of Poseidon/Neptune. These figures seem a mockery of the word "god." Readers, whether delighted or bored, have remained safe from any serious cosmic model that might collide with traditional association with godhood. The Homeric Olympians endorse for human beings a moral code including slavery, lying, seizing treasure and filling one's belly by any means, No family of petulant, capricious, squabbling immortals—gods with a decidedly small "g"—could appear viable as a spiritual resource. Ascribing awe to such figures seems as impossible for Westerners to take seriously as the power of Anansi the Spider in the lives of the Ashanti people.

But the Greeks did have another, more serious, level of worship, one that offered them comfort, security, and a means to answer eternal questions, the rituals of the Eleusinian Mysteries. It is notably ironic that the trivialization of the Olympians, and therefore ancient Greek religion, was facilitated by the fact that those worshipers, having vowed secrecy to protect the profound and sophisticated Eleusinian rites, held fast to their prohibitive vows and left no written record, Even today we still know little of these ceremonies beyond their being based on the cosmic story of the search by Demeter/Ceres, goddess of grain, for her daughter Persephone/Proserpina, after the younger was abducted by the lord of the underworld, Hades/Pluto.

For the past several decades, studies have been under way looking into the use of grain-derived psychedelic substances in these rituals, akin to those used in parts of Mexico. The basis of these studies is the idea that the goal of Eleusinian worship was not only a transcending but also a transformative religious ecstasy that these substances generate (Wasson). In any case, this well-secreted domestic story, without a role for a creator, gives an accounting for the seasons and their effect on crops. While Persephone is in the Underworld, vegetation ceases. Her mother, in desperation and on behalf of the earth as well as out of her personal grief, manages a compromise at last with Zeus's help, to divide the daughter's time above and below the earth. The story could not have ended in any other way.

Religious conservatism ruled scholarship in the Western world well into the twentieth century, so that scholars have viewed other people's sacred stories either as curiosities or as a barbarous clambering toward our enlightened state. It is not entirely a battle won. The textbook titled *The Short Story and the Oral Tradition*, by Paul C. Sherr, 1971, prefaces a creation story with this remark: "The ancient pagans, not having the information on [the creation of the world] which we derive from the pages of Scripture, had their own way of telling the story" (80). Pagans and heathens, with their negative connotations, are currently defined in dictionaries as subscribers to beliefs other than the monotheist triad of Christianity, Judaism, and Islam.

Malinowski, despite depending on such terms as "savage" and "primitive," distinguished himself in appreciating the sophisticated ways of worship of the Pacific Trobriand Islanders he lived with. Had other scholars looked as boldly at the numerous parallels between the quaint pagan stories and Western received truths, they would have been forced to an impossible position: Christianity would have to be reduced to one of the many ways people in the world believe. Other faiths would have to be elevated to valid religions.

That would mean allowing the viability, for example, of what many Hawaiians today believe, that the goddess Pelée manifests her emotions through volcanic eruption. Visitors to Nepal's Kathmandu Valley would have to take seriously a young goddess who represents wisdom and spirituality coming to her balcony every afternoon—she will be replaced when she reaches puberty. One would have to recognize that the cows wandering streets and alleys of India with impunity are as sacred to some people as a crucifix is to others.

A Roman Catholic would set aside distaste and bafflement when the taking of communion is posed as an example of a living ritual along with the placating of demons by sacrificial offerings in Bali. In both cases, the ritual is partner to myth and doctrine in belief-systems. How many One Truths can there be?

Aldous Huxley addresses this problem in his introductory essay to the *Bhagavad-Gita*, later expanded into a book, "The Perennial Philosophy," in which he characterizes the great religions as possessing corners of the Truth, like the four blind men in the fable, each touching one part of the elephant and interpreting it as the whole. The one who touches the tail might say that God is like a rope, and the one who feels the side might conclude that God is like a wall. All believers, Huxley maintains, share the notion of a divine level with whom they can aspire to communicate in the hope of a response. Only the forms differ. Pope Pius XII was willing to acknowledge the creation story as myth or allegory when he accepted physicists' demonstrations of the earth's historical age. It is likely that the physical sciences carry more authority with the Church than the social sciences. Mythological elements in the life of Jesus that appear as well in other belief-system stories preceding his lifetime, such as the motif of the savior's return from underworld after three days, can be daunting. It is difficult, too, for many to accept the classifying of Biblical scripture with animist tales like the African dung-beetle's creation of the world.

The point about science leads to the second giant blocking the understanding of myth.

A perusal of mythological scholarship reveals that the methodology is itself a product and tool of a categorical view of reality. With the authority of scientific terminology and procedure in the era of technology, scholars in sociology, psychology, and anthropology have modeled both vocabularies and processes after the prestigious structures of science. Social scientists have from their introduction into the academy sought professional legitimacy through disciplines that would merit university departments, government grants, and a voice in history. What results is discussion of myth in the jargon of a narrow "science."

Carl Jung suggests a further reason for the "cloak of so-called scientific understanding" when he maintains that we in the west fear that "an understanding that reaches the feelings might allow contact with the foreign spirit to become a serious experience" (*Secret of the Golden Flower*, 77). Dr. Jung, impressed with the Chinese idea of the Tao, especially its dualities, yin and yang, and the anima and animus in conflict, wrote with humility about a European trying to comprehend from within a limited culture what he recognizes are valuable ideas. To see how seriously an educated modern Westerner may be moved to take a foreign spirit, one can cite Laurens van der Post's *Lost World of the Kalahari*, in which he finds himself writing a letter to the spirits of Southwest Africa's Tsodilo Hills in order to get his cameras and Land-Rover operating again. It works.

Literary critics have much to learn from anthropologists but cannot get through the latters' bad prose. (Malinowski, an exception, shares Joseph Conrad's apparent blessing of having spoken Polish into adulthood and learned English late.) Left to their own traditions, the professional readers and commentators long made a cult of Aristotle's *Poetics*, then were phallicized in the 1950's by the Freudians, then symbolized by the Jungians in the 1960's, and eventually, near century's end, fell in love with signifiers as objects in themselves and came to see themselves as enlightened exploders of the content or referent—the signified. Unready to acknowledge this approach as a belief-system in itself, they associate the term "myth-maker" with poets like Yeats, honor the classics as repositories of allusions, and otherwise disgorge myth of its anthropological vibrancy and social context.

"Myth" is a popular word in the currency of literary critics. They have avenged themselves on Thomas Love Peacock, who, in the nineteenth century, in response to Percy Bysshe Shelley's eloquent claims, attacked the poetic factor as useless and unprogressive. He accused poets of staking claim to *poesis* for the arts alone, as if fantasy, reverie, inspiration, and subjectivity are not also the province of an Albert Einstein, a Thomas Jefferson, a Jonas Salk—even a Plato, an artist who banned artists from his ideal realm in *The Republic.* Mircea Eliade points out in *Myth and Reality* that myths share with science and philosophy the subordination of individual experiences. They achieve this subordination, he maintains, by transmitting "paradigmatic models established by Supernatural Beings," while science and philosophy do so by transmitting models of reality that are "transpersonal" ideas. All of this model-making distances a person from his "historical moment" (138).

It may be most useful to consider myths in terms of what they do, that is, how they serve their society. It is for others—chiefly folklorists—to probe how certain patterns of stories came to appear from Alaska to Africa, as the Snow White tale does. Here we can consider (1) that people want to tell and hear stories about eternal matters, (2) that creeds are best conveyed through story form, and (3) that these stories carry values about behavior that knit societies together. It may be true that when one's feet are covered with leather, the whole world is covered with leather, but the premise of this book is that one can stand embedded within a culture and yet see its correspondences with universals in others.

Chapter Seven

Communication: Prayer and Sacrifice

TWO GENERAL modes in which people practice their beliefs are esoteric (within) and exoteric (external). The esoteric worshiper experiences and reflects on what can be described as a divine connection that in itself is fulfilling, inspiring, completing. One finds today contemplative Buddhist monks, cloistered Catholic nuns, and Hindu and Moslem ascetics, their transcending experience through prayer or meditation being the consummation of worship, even of existence.

Most practitioners of religion in the Western world are exoteric. For them it is important, even compelling, to communicate to others what is happening within them spiritually. A critical part of their belief, then, is to fortify it with agreement.

The various religions behave differently in this respect. Some, like Jainism and Judaism, discourage conversion to their society and practices. An aspiring convert to orthodox or conservative Judaism is required to study and be tested at length before being accepted into the community. More familiar in Western culture, however, is the urge of religious groups to disseminate what they are convinced is divine truth. The term "evangelism" means the spreading of the gospel, or the good news about Christ as redeemer.

The reasons for the eagerness to persuade others to one's own belief are many, and not only political, but apparently the energy aroused by such activity reinforces one's personal fervor. It is also a way of participating actively in a belief-community by creating new boundaries and expressions. Mainly it is a way to keep talking to oneself while talking to others, as a recovering substance-abuser might constantly strengthen himself or herself by means of earnest helpfulness, and a teacher of mythology keeps learning in every lecture more about mythology than before he or she had to communicate about it.

Even when one takes a solitary esoteric path or a vow of silence, the bond with others supports the belief through a community of certainty. The context of familiar stories, songs, incense, drumbeats, bells, costumes, and chants adds up to a code by which members relate to one another on the basis of their common history and traditions. Often these rituals involve the separation of men and women as an unquestioned necessity grounded in nature.

The community's treatment of women varies dramatically, from, at one end, subservience and denial of access to means and property, to, at the other end, power that is matrilocal (using the territory of the wife's kin group) and/or matrilinear (tracing ancestral descent through the mother's line). In some systems a female is either herself the creator or a partner in creating the world and its conditions. In Japanese mythology, when the demi-god Izana-gi pursues his wife Izana-mi to the underworld after she dies, and looks at her disfigured face, her rage leads to her bringing death to humankind. His resourceful idea to supplant the dead with new population saves the human race. This couple, then, are accountable for the basic condition of our lives. African tales often make women accountable, through their excessive curiosity, meddling, or gossip, for massive calamities, like eclipses, and even death.

Because of generational repetition, women are at least as active as men in maintaining rituals that harm women. For example, the practice of female genital mutilation is today vigorously enforced by mothers who have themselves suffered the traumatic and medically discountenanced ordeal, as a means to ensure their daughters' acceptability for marriage. Resulting injuries, aside from mortality, can ironically lead to a husband's banishing the damaged, incontinent, woman. Whatever its basis of origin, the long-standing practice still remains resistant to challenge.

Traditions, especially regarding the sexes, resist modification. In the Bible's Pentateuch (Leviticus 12), the Lord tells Moses that after delivering a male child a woman is unclean for one week and banned from the sanctuary for thirty-three days, but if she bears a female child, she is unclean for two weeks and banned from the sanctuary for sixty-six days. These rituals convey in ordinary daily life the doctrine of lesser worth of females.

Menstruation plays a role in North American tales of temporary banishment from household activities, and it was only in 2005 that the Nepalese government ruled as illegal the custom of confining women to the cowshed for four days during their periods. Isolation during menstruation was a long-standing practice in Russia. The inevitable consequence is a female person's feeling of shame. Similarly, the caste system adhered to primarily in Hinduism predetermines groups to lives of shame, with the consolation of a religion that stresses acceptance of one's social level, no matter how demeaning, as a platform to perform good deeds. Clearly, these traditions are so entrenched as the community's eternal truth that individual persons have no opportunity to instigate change or exception.

Two traditional codes that bind and strengthen a community in worship are prayer and sacrifice, both entreaties for divine favor. Numerous studies have been and are being conducted on the efficacy of prayer for oneself or for others, even for animals. Results are controversial, but it is apparent that whether they do heal or not, deliver or not, the value lies in the praying. The ritual of praying naturally enlivens hope, but is also an articulation and stretching toward the divine. While individual praying may be the purest form of worship, praying in a group is a direct and powerful means of bonding with others.

What do people yearn for? Their well-being and that of their families are of most immediate concern, along with victory over environmental hazards and alien hostility. Illness and disease have always imperiled survival and prompted measures to ward them off, treatment being a form of prayer. Medicine's relation to ritual has a long and rich history that can be touched on only briefly here.

Asclepius may have at one time been historically a physician, but became a demi-god in the Greek and Roman pantheons, as son of Apollo, father of six healing daughters including Panacea, and storied practitioner of the healing arts. His name is today part of the medical profession's Hippocratic oath. According to Plato's account, Socrates just before his death referred to having consulted him. Lore has it that he was cast into the galaxy as punishment for bringing the dead back to life, an act, like Prometheus's gift of fire, guaranteed to win sympathy among human beings.

Especially talented men or women designated in communities as healers, medicine-men, or "witch-doctors" have worked for millennia, at least back to Neolithic times—no one knows how far back in history shamanism extends, for example—through communication with spirits. When they fail to achieve a cure, of course, they can explain that other, more powerful, spirits opposed them. But as with prayer, the alternative to aspiration is despair. Asclepius reportedly succeeded through the efficacy of ritual in overcoming bodily afflictions. Healers like him often work in association with animals regarded as sacred, especially the snake. Snakes, sinuous and speedy, are particularly suitable to myth and ritual in being of double aspect, or paradoxical. They can be either deadly or curative, and in some cases both.

The prevalence of snakes worldwide in myths and rituals has reflected an ambivalence toward them, but they are invariably regarded as powerful. In the Genesis narrative, part of the Lord's meting out of punishment after the Eden violation is to condemn the serpent forever to be loathed by human beings. Similarly the worm in the Hittite tribe was condemned by the wisdom-god to crawl without limbs, only after it had won the boon of delving in human teeth.

The physical property of snakes to shed their skin provides a natural suggestion of regeneration, no doubt one reason why in many of the world's cultures the snake's power is benign, or at least can be negotiated by proper ritual into collaboration. Today in Northeast Arizona the Hopi tribe continues to perform their time-honored snake-dance, participants holding live rattle-snakes in their teeth. Asclepian healing sites were said to have non-poisonous snakes crawling around the floor near the sick. The emblem of Asclepius is a snake coiled around a staff (not to be confused with the caduceus, linked with Hermes). Medieval coins show a crucified Christ on one side and a snake coiled around a crucifix on the other.

If one knows nothing else about India, one knows about the venomous cobra's tendency to be mesmerized and therefore rendered harmless by music from a flute. Snakeskins and other parts of snakes have been used medicinally in China for more than two thousand years, and still are, to the extent that some species are nearing extinction. Traditionally in Japan it was regarded as good luck for the household to have a snake living in one's attic, not only to kill mice and other small creatures but also to ward off bad luck and illness.

Along with prayer, another code that has appeared through time to bind communities to their doctrine is sacrifice. There are, of course, non-religious and semi-religious sacrifices, like those made in war for one's country, but the focus here is on worship. In that context, sacrifice, like prayer, is a form of negotiation.

The religious practice of sacrifice depends on the attributing of human personality and motives to deities. That is, in order for whatever one sacrifices to have value, the deity or deities would necessarily share the same language as the worshiper. If the deity does not eat meat, he or she must at least be able to imagine what is being forfeited by the gift of meat, often the very finest specimen of the cattle. What the deity would conceivably do with it is not a consideration. What does matter is that the one who offers it will suffer its loss. That forfeiture can be of nourishment, as in fasting, or physical comfort, as in self-flagellation

What does the supplicant expect in return? Primarily, survival, but in particular, advantages immediately at hand. When the Achaeans sacrifice Agamemnon's daughter Iphigenia at Aulis, the purpose is to persuade the gods to release the winds so that the stalled fleet can launch its assault on Troy. Supplicants, not knowing exactly what the deities desire, have to proceed according to what they themselves would most cherish.

And so we get virgins tossed from cliffs.

In fact, Biblical references to human sacrifice (2 Kings: 23.10) and exhortations to end it, and South American pre-Columbian graphic images of the practice, leave no doubt that it existed. Even today, martyrdom particularly among Moslems is a sacrifice as well as a kind of prayer to Allah, the Supreme Being. The family and community are likely to regard this sacrifice as cause for celebration in view of their belief in an afterworld rich in rewards.

Sometimes, riches go in the other direction. Ancient Egyptians designed elaborate send-offs for their royalty, like King Tutankhamen in the 14th century B.C.E. The belief was that royal persons were destined for an afterworld where they would become gods and benefactors of those remaining behind. Their ritually mummified bodies were accompanied not only by favorite objects and furniture, but also by the bodies of servants and members of the royal court. These may have been devoted volunteers for the sacrifice, or they may have had nothing to say in the arrangements.

Pelée, the violent-tempered female deity of the Hawaiian Big Island's Mount Kilauea, has not been officially a sacrifice-demanding deity since Hawaii became Christian in the early nineteenth century. Yet she exacts deference to her dignity regularly through fiercely intimidating eruptions.

Sacrifice is usually a bargain with a partner who is not talking, just acting. Of course the anthropomorphic Lord in the Old Testament does talk, on occasion thunderously, as in the Book of Job. Probably the most famous sacrifice in Western culture did not actually take place. Isaac's near-slaughter by his father Abraham (Genesis 22:1-19) is described as a test, illustrating the extent to which the Lord requires absolute fidelity. The fact that Isaac is Abraham's only son, born when Abraham was a century old, further drives home the severity of the test and Abraham's success in passing it.

What is the alternative to sacrifice? To much of the world, none has seemed available. In a twentieth-century Graham Greene novel, *The End of the Affair*, the woman protagonist sacrifices her love affair in the belief that her act will spare the life of her lover. She projects a bargain in terms of her Christian belief and conversation with God.

The gods have the power. Humankind has none. But if the gods are anything like human beings, at least enough to understand their language, they too must want something. In Oregon's Klamath Yurok tribe, according to Theodora Kroeber, the perfect dance—stamping on the earth—is a ritual required by gods and nature to keep the world in balance. With this annual dance the Yurok are exercising power in their own survival. Benjamin Hunningher in *The Origin of the Theater* maintains that religion itself began with the ritual of dance, when early society recognized that gods looked favorably on precise performances, and so a holy bargain and dialogue began.

The practice of sacrifice, however, is not such a cold, mechanical transaction. The supplicant gains not only the anticipation of a favorable response but also the certain knowledge that the group looks approvingly on the activity, which they deem as right, proper (Homer's "seemly"), holy, that is, the will of the gods. Like prayer, then, sacrifice takes on the double value of communication with the divine and with society.

Chapter Eight

Circe: The Intersection of Myth and Literature

MYTH, OR story, naturally comes to us in words. Often the narrative is simple, even episodic, burnished by generations of repetition. But sometimes it flourishes in the hands of an artist whose craft transforms it from a simple tale to a gem for the ages. One of the distinctions Chapter 4 gives between myth and other kinds of stories is mythological literature. Homer, whoever he (or she) was, is unsurpassed as a narrative artist who shaped the material he inherited into a literary masterpiece. His tale of Circe in the *Odyssey* is a noteworthy example of how fittingly the skills of literary criticism can apply in a study of that epic.

The traditions about Circe that Homer inherited, like those about any mythical figure, had to change in his telling. Bards are bound to alter traditional material as they follow their own designs. And whether or not Homer was blind, or a woman, or a committee, the *Odyssey* text discloses a Circe quite distinct from the nasty portrayals in texts both before and since that epic's composition. Inasmuch as Homer is the most extensive literary source of her portrayal, it is striking that all the favorable qualities Homer's text attributes to her evaporate in dictionaries, encyclopedias, poems, and psychiatric allusions to her. It seems that the compelling image of men transmuted into beasts, the stuff of nightmares, overrides Homer's carefully generous rendering.

The Circe story in the epic is not merely Homer's narrative. It has two lives. In Thousand-and-One-Nights fashion, it is a tale with which Homer's character Odysseus spellbinds his hosts, the Phaeacians of the island of Scherie. As he recites, he wants two things: to return to his home in Ithaca, and to return there rich. By the time he has finished, the enthralled hosts give him treasure and safe-passage to the home he has not seen for nineteen years. Homer wants his listeners—us—to grasp and possibly duplicate how rapt Odysseus's listeners are. During a break in the hero-guest's recitation, Homer shows that Phaeacian audience overwhelmed. How the story is put together, then, derives from Odysseus' rhetorical purposes as well as Homer's. What are some of the strategies that produce a benign portrait of Circe?

In our time her name has become a term for a fatally sexy witch. In *Man and his Symbols*, edited by Carl Jung, we find: "In the minds of many people, the pig is closely associated to dirty sexuality. (Circe, for example, changed the men who desired her into swine). . . . The pig-like animal of the [patient's] dream connotes bestiality and lustfulness—as in the myth of Circe, who turned men into swine" (Jacobi, 282-3). According to the *American Heritage Dictionary*, Circe is "an enchantress described in the *Odyssey* who detains Odysseus for a year and turns his men into swine." The sequence here tells a lie. Before the year begins Circe has already returned the men to human form, once Odysseus has asked her to. The "detaining" is also misleading and applies rather to Calypso in another episode. Odysseus so ardently wishes to stay with Circe that his crew members have to persuade him to leave.

Circe is called "pitiless" by Robert Graves in *The White Goddess* (502), and "dehumanizing" by Howard Porter in his synopsis for the Palmer (Bantam) translation (23), and Michael Grant writes, "Circe is predatory, but Calypso is affectionate" (80). In Homer's ethos an affection that impedes a man's return to home and purpose is poisonous. A recent anthology lists Circe with Delilah in a section labeled "The Temptress," with Circe labeled Destructive and the "opposite of the figure of the protective earth mother" (Burrows 423). All these portrayals bear little resemblance to Homer's character.

That Homer knew tales of a sorceress called *Kirke* (a hooping-in, from falconry), we may suppose from Hesiod's reference to her. But Homer altered that figure into a benefactor for Odysseus, unsurpassed even by his unwavering sponsor Athena in devotion and generosity. Once Odysseus becomes identified, shortly after they meet, she swears an oath of trustworthiness and becomes in all respects a kindly figure, an intelligent companion who, unlike the selfish Calypso, never clings, but takes all her pleasure from the hero's comfort and success. In sum, she is the opposite of the "opposite of the figure of the protective earth mother." Only at the outset of her episode does she conform to the folklore tradition, and even then Homer's diction downplays the wickedness.

Circe's dwelling, surrounded by trees, sits in the middle of an island named Aeaea, from *gaia*, "the land," where she sings and weaves at her loom. By tradition she is daughter of Helios (a version of the sun) and Perse, aunt to sorceress Medea, the child of her brother Aietes. Her reputation would hardly profit from such connections. And so what Homer does is omit them. For his purposes, she has no past and no future, but seems waiting to be happened on, or to happen.

Circe at her loom calls to mind the pastime of Penelope, Helen, Hector's wife Andromache, and, pertinently, Arete, the Phaeacian queen hearing Odysseus' tale. The woven object is salient in Greco-Roman tales—Penelope's shroud for Odysseus's father Laertes, Arachne's trenchant satire on the gods, Philomela's desperate message to her sister Procne—but as Circe and Calypso sing at work at their looms they are subject-less. Their producing merely blank lovely fabric is in keeping with Homer's depiction of deities, who are immortal, mimicking human activities empty of human passions and motives. But Homer makes Circe distinctly compassionate among immortals.

The story of Circe as Homer wanted Odysseus to want to tell it, from Book X to Book XII, describes an immortal who, once she has learned who Odysseus is, becomes entirely generous. This portrayal departs not only from the folklore caricature but also from Odysseus' own reference in his boastful introduction to the Phaeacian court in IX. "The divine Calypso," he tells them, "certainly did her best to keep me yonder in her cavern home because she wished to be my wife, and with the same object Circe, the Aeaean witch, detained me in her castle; but never for a moment did they win my heart" (Rieu, 139-140).

According to his fuller account of Circe, Odysseus here misrepresents her. Why? Two strategies underpin Odysseus' rhetoric. First, the king and queen of Scherie generally, and their daughter Nausicaa specifically, have made it clear that Odysseus would be a welcome husband for her; he will have to use tact to elicit treasure and safe-conduct from his hosts while at the same time refusing their daughter. The royal family will not be insulted if two goddesses have similarly failed to divert him from his goal. Second, immediately before and after his boast of female attention in IX he asserts that a man's homeland and family are what are sweetest to him.

In the epic which has everything to do with Odysseus' return (*"nostos"*), Homer depicts the Phaeacians as idyllically civilized, consequently esteeming love for home. Odysseus uses his undifferentiated examples of Calypso and Circe to show the degree of temptation one must at times withstand. It would not serve to distinguish between the one who tried to possess him and the one who did not.

Odysseus as well as Homer is drawing upon his listeners' broad acquaintance with mythical tradition. Ancient tales about the sorceress who changed men into swine—and possibly other animals—abounded, although accounts of what befell her vary widely. Pre-Homeric minstrel tradition, reflected in the *Theogony* and the *Telegonia,* gives Odysseus and Circe two sons, one of whom slays Odysseus in Ithaca. (Apollodorus later has Odysseus' son Telemachus marry Circe after his father's death [Loeb, ii, 303]. The Alexandrian Apollonius Rhodias has Circe exposing corpses on her island for birds to eat [ii, 1260; iv, 246], and purifying the Argonauts for the murder of her nephew, Medea's brother [iv, 557, 659-717]. Later stories of Circe, mostly Roman, stress her evil, as in Ovid's Picus story, in which she transforms her beloved into a woodpecker for loving another [*Metamorphoses,* XIV, 320 ff.].)

Rhys Carpenter maintains that Homer's source was a fairy tale (18-20). Carpenter observes that Homer forgets to have the hero eat the moly-plant—but the herb as amulet could suffice. He says, too, that Homer omits the fate of the wolves and lions. Restored, however, they would spoil the plot, and, importantly, they are not Ithacans. He notices, too, that Homer's forest setting is European, but there were (and still are) wooded areas in Greece. There do, in the end, appear to be two discrete Circes, one in popular tale that survives in later literary references, and the other Homer's variation. When editors refer to Homer's Circe as the "opposite of the figure of the protective earth mother," they confuse two representations of the character.

Circe's name occurs first in the *Odyssey* when the hero refers in VIII (l. 448) to her having taught him the art of tying complicated knots. This reference contributes to Odysseus' image as dependent on women for his survival, his knowledge, and his hopes, and it accords with the later detailed story of Circe's munificence. When the Phaeacian Queen advises this stranger to secure his treasure against thieves, he uses a subtle knot that Queenly (Homer's word *potnia* conveys reverence) Circe had "taught his mind." By mentioning Circe, Homer lets his listeners know that the hero, who has not yet given his story to the Phaeacians, has yet a good tale to tell—to both the fictional and the actual audience. More vitally, he plants Circe in the narrative as a teaching and therefore a benevolent influence. In the next lines Odysseus recalls his debts to both Calypso, who gave him steaming baths, and Princess Nausicaa, who saved his life.

The passage highlights women who aid the hero—Queen Arete, Circe, Calypso, and Nausicaa—pointing out Odysseus' dependence as aging survivor on the guest-host convention and the good will of (female) others.

Absent in Odysseus' account to the Phaeacians, IX through XII, is Athena, the deity who through the rest of the twenty-four books is faithfully available as mentor and guide, celebrant of his subtlety. Homer may have meant the shrewdly political Odysseus to conceal his indebtedness and closeness to her, an enemy of Poseidon, patron and ancestor of the Phaeacians.

But Homer the tale-spinner himself had reasons to omit her, chiefly that the lofty Olympians, except for boundaryless Hermes, do not properly fit in the world of folklore and magic that Odysseus's tale occupies. All the way to the Aethiopes, enemies in the epic are mortal men or gods whose ancestry and strength can be measured, not monsters, cannibals, or sea-sirens. Athena belongs in the cognitive realm, not the phantasmagorical realm of Odysseus' tale. Yet Homer shows in Book VIII that even in the absence of Athena, women—a queen, a sorceress, a lesser goddess, a princess—are carrying Odysseus through.

And Circe's gifts are prodigious.

In Odysseus' tale, X to XII, she bestows on him a gift that corresponds to the harmonizing influence of Queen Arete ("Excellence") on her idyllic society. It is within the Circe episode that Odysseus reaches the apex of familial closeness with his crewmen. Before he and they meet her, and promptly after they leave her, the men are in conflict with their leader—they are inferior, alien. In fact, in XII they slay Hyperion's sacred cattle—an immeasurably costly violation—while Odysseus sleeps. But while they are within Circe's sphere (hoop) of influence, Homer makes the devotion between leader and crew so tender that he portrays it in maternal rather than brotherly images.

Outside that magical sphere, Odysseus says it is his "fools of" men, not he, who commit the costly excesses after the sack of the Cicones in the first adventure. The three men who reconnoiter the country of the Lotus Eaters partake of food that erases "thought of home"—Odysseus's most compelling virtue to his audience. Because loss of memory of home equals removal of context for valor (manliness), he puts the three in chains. Forgetfulness of home is mutiny.

In the Cyclops adventure his men depend entirely on the hero's wit. They share none of his courage, and their indistinctness as persons allows us to tolerate their being devoured and vomited up in fragments. The surviving crew caution Odysseus not to taunt the Cyclops, but he is too excited about himself and does so, with calamitous results.

In the Aeolus episode the crew steals treasure (what is more precious at sea than wind?) while Odysseus sleeps. Failure of trust, more than greed, causes most of the fleet to perish. All this precedes the influence Circe will exert.

The greatly diminished crew that arrive at Circe's Aeaea have seen all their comrades not only killed but killed for food by monstrous folk, yet even in this scene of grief Odysseus is apart from the others. While the men lie on the beach exhausted and distressed for two days, Odysseus feels singularly god-gifted when a huge stag appears for him to kill and nourish them.

After their feast Odysseus makes the remarkable announcement that on this island, with its wisp of smoke right in the middle, they are literally disoriented. "East and West mean nothing to us here" (160). The crew's emotional state is reflected in this dis-orientation, which for sailors is disintegration. Is Homer expressing the anomalousness of the Circe experience, as a threshold to the venture into Hades, at the theological center of the epic?

Of course, her wickedness is there. At first she makes the men comfortable and drugs their food. There are two separate steps to her sorcery, a fact that most accounts of the *Odyssey* overlook. First, her drug produces the same awful effect of the Lotus Eaters, "to make them lose all memory of their native land" (161). Then, after they eat, she uses

her wand to transform them into swine in appearance only. This section of the story is sketchy. There is no hint of what Circe intends to do with the creatures, no evidence that they are to be eaten, or why these become swine rather than wolves and lions—perhaps only for Homer to keep them confined at close quarters for their dramatic release, and to distinguish them from the others. Circe gives them food appropriate to their form, and although they weep, the drug of forgetfulness abates their pain. While one can hardly attribute kindness to Circe here, Homer and Odysseus blur her most destructive moment, and her menacing function occupies a brief and mechanical portion of her story. Compare Ovid's chilling first-person account in the *Metamorphoses* of a Circe victim's conversion to pig features.

Odysseus has received from Hermes a counter-drug to subdue Circe, the moly (probably a lily-leek), whose nullifying power appears to lie less in its properties than in the knowledge of its effect and of rites of conduct. Precise ritual knowledge is magic: Hermes predicts every move of Circe's, and that she will abide by an oath.

Thusly armed, Odysseus resists Circe's drug and wand. Tearful at his knees, she recognizes Odysseus, whom Hermes had warned her to expect. As with the Cyclops and the King of Scherie, Odysseus becomes prophecy fulfilled. At this moment of submission Circe invites Odysseus to bed, "so that in love and sleep we may learn to trust one another" (164). One can expect the word "trust" on the lips of a traditional sorceress not to be honored, but not so with the character Homer creates. Once Odysseus elicits from her the oath of no-more-mischief, there is no character in the epic whose word is more reliable. Contrary to his fear that she would un-man him, she is unsurpassed in strengthening him.

As they go to bed Homer discreetly shifts to nature-nymphs decorating the palace and heating the bath water. But after the leader's bath and olive-oil rub, his men preoccupy him. His disinterest in food (exceptional in Homer) and his introspection baffle Circe. And then, the instant she learns he wants the men released, she uses another drug or salve to restore them to an appearance even better than before. When the men and Odysseus weep together, the goddess is touched, and from this point Homer's portrait of Circe is unqualifiedly sympathetic.

While Homer laces his *Iliad* battles with similes of farm and home, in the *Odyssey* such similes are infrequent. Yet when Odysseus tells of reuniting with his forlorn shipmates, Homer has him use two successive similes. The first is extraordinary in that it makes Odysseus a mother, in an image of calves rushing to welcome home the cows. He reinforces this image with the men being "as deeply moved as if they had reached their homeland and were standing in the streets of their own town in rugged Ithaca" (166). Homer turns to the very target that Odysseus and his crew are bent upon. Nowhere else in the epic do such tender emotions exist between Odysseus and his men as on Circe's island.

During the reunion between the men from the ship and those restored from swine-form, Circe delivers a speech abounding in understanding of their sorrows. She concludes, "But now, I want to see you enjoying your food and putting down your wine, till you are once more the men you were when first you sailed from your homes in rugged Ithaca" (168). Her famed sorcery, then, loses its danger and becomes positive: her gift will be their original strength. Odysseus' story proper gives no support to his prefatory comment (in IX) that Circe's motive in detaining him was marriage. And the labels "pitiless" and "predatory" become misrepresentations.

After a year of feasting, the crew has to remind the hero of their homeward purpose. Their subordinated status eroded by comforts, they reproach him simply as a comrade. The leader who had saved them from forgetfulness-of-purpose has himself yielded to it. Odysseus reminds Circe of her vow to send him home, tactfully ascribing impatience to his men only. Although no such promise is in the text, Circe responds efficiently, without Calypso's balking and whining. There is, though, an element of bargaining. She describes the journey he must take before she can send him home: to the Dead, to consult the seer Teiresias. She instructs him about taboos and ritual sacrifices, describing, as did Hermes their own meeting, with the predictive exactness of sorcery folklore.

Homer keeps Circe both human and immortal. The balance is impressive. The way he conceives of making her human is to make her "womanly." As a woman Circe dresses Odysseus and herself attractively for his departure, while as deity she vanishes without farewell ceremony, after providing the animals the sacrifices will require. Though she looks and communicates like a human being, Odysseus says, the goddess sends a favorable breeze (XII, 157). And at each step in the terrifying visit to the dead, Odysseus is fortified in the control of taboos through knowledge from Circe.

Suddenly the tale breaks off, and Homer brings his audience of Phaeacians back to the attention of his larger audience. In an interlude of a few lines, Queen Arete secures the King's indulgence for their guest. In both inner and outer stories a woman is carrying Odysseus through. The anthology that classifies Circe under "The Temptress" omits everything after Book X, including her favorable breeze that takes the ship to its destination. But Homer has more work for this temptress.

The crew's return to Circe's home from the realm of the Dead contains the joys attending a safe homecoming. Now Dawn is red in the East: disorientation has ended. Circe, all decked out, greets them with servants carrying food. She is jubilant over their feat of having visited the Dead. In contrast with Calypso, who offers the hero immortality if only he will remain with her, Circe unaccountably declares that after only a day's food and rest they are to sail away at dawn. The haste seems to serve nothing so well as Homer's need for momentum, but Circe's portrayal profits.

At night, with the crew settled, Circe takes Odysseus by the hand, not to entice him, but to listen. Her conduct anticipates Penelope's wifely behavior after the couple's reunion in XXIII: Circe invites him to "sit down and tell her all my news as she lay beside me" (190). His report concluded, she spends the rest of the night until dawn carefully detailing navigational cues and the hazards before him—the Sirens, Scylla and Charybdis, and the Thrinacie. She is serious, chiding, fearful on his behalf, far from a pitiless, predatory "opposite of earth-mothers."

Circe's directions concerning the Sirens constitute a remarkable gift. It would suffice for all the men to plug their ears with beeswax, but Circe helps Odysseus to become initiated—the one man to have endured the ordeal—by suggesting that he listen to the Sirens when his men have bound him. These instructions, besides making Odysseus a superman, rest delicately upon trust that his men will not accede to his pleadings to be untied. These same men had violated the Aeolian bag of winds and will later outrage Hyperion, causing their own deaths and leaving Odysseus all alone. But Circe knows that the crew is presently in such harmony with Odysseus that the experiment can work.

She is mentor, nurturer, harmonizer. Yet when departure-time arrives at dawn, there is no farewell scene. There has been no languishing passion, like Calypso's, or spousal speculation, like Nausicaa's. Sex, once it has fixed trust, has been matter-of-fact and incidental to the visit; the narrative always gives precedence to other comforts. True, Odysseus, with the queen and princess in his audience, would play down the erotic aspects of his stay with the sorceress, but Homer's broader purposes are served as well. The concern that Circe demonstrates, the blessings and warnings, are precisely what the chaste Athena gives Odysseus in the rest of the *Odyssey*. Athena, however, is not native to the domain of magic. Hermes alone of the Olympians may enter, so impurely Olympian, the consummate mediator between worlds, who in this epic might be any faery figure versed in magic and herbology.

The one-dimensional sorceress whom we first meet routinely weaving pointless gossamer is word-woven into bountiful divinity and woman, her powers mobilized to a purpose. She slips away a second time without awaiting thanks from the home-bound hero who, though still very much Odysseus, is more sophisticated now. The witch who could change men to less-than-men has introduced him to the mysteries that make him more-than-man.

Through the art of Odysseus the storyteller, as Homer's craft fashions him, Circe gets transformed from a mannequin, a stereotype in folklore tradition, to a developed character, a personality who enjoys focusing her energies to assist in an ennobling project. The narrator Odysseus, dazzling the Phaeacian court, embroiders and omits according to his motives, but of course it is Homer who has transformed all.

Chapter Nine

The *Oresteia:* The Intersection of Myth and Politics

IN THE 1960 Jules Dassin film set in modern Greece, "Never on Sunday," the prostitute protagonist copes with the sadness of classical tragedies by persuading herself that the characters don't really suffer and die in the end, they all go to the beach. She is able to rationalize this way because the actors leave the stage intact. But she may have been on to something.

We are fortunate to have the plays, thanks to the third-century C.E. scholars in Alexandria, Egypt, who copied, catalogued, and preserved a selection of manuscripts of indescribable treasures from the Greece of seven centuries earlier. Because of these archivists we have at least some (about one-hundred-twenty) of the tragedies, which are components of mostly lost three-play sets, or trilogies, by Aeschylus, Sophocles and Euripides. Except for the Aeschylus trilogy, the *Oresteia,* composed and first performed in 458 B.C.E., all the rescued tragedies familiar to the west are in fact incomplete—thirds of trilogies—and cannot easily be identified as first, second, or third play in the sequence.

What leads modern audiences to believe that tragedy (literally "goat song," probably named for the earliest prizes) means catastrophe is the incompleteness of each work. In Sophocles' *Oedipus Rex*, the best known of the collection, Queen Jocasta kills herself and the king blinds and exiles himself. Euripides' Medea slays her children; Sophocles' Antigone and Creon's wife and son end up slain. Or go to the beach.

But Aeschylus's full trilogy concludes, after two plays immersed in catastrophe, not only in resolution but also in a spirit of political jubilation. In the same manner that Shakespeare would later finish his most painful tragedies, Aeschylus returned a battered cosmos to order. Again, the ABC of myth is Anything But Chaos.

Viewing the trilogy through this book's proposed model of belief-system comprised of story, ritual, and doctrine, one easily sees the inherited story, largely derived from the University of Homer, and its relation to ritual. But Aeschylus has done something radical, by bending doctrine in a new direction. Some background should help clarify why.

Modern readers and audiences approach the classical tragedies without the political assumptions that underlie the story and are key to much of its power. As with all literature, traditional material provides context for the artist, who in turn renders the traditions palpable and lasting. But in the *Oresteia* the traditional material was and is dense in politics as well as mythology. To appreciate how richly political the Greek tragedies were, and in particular this trilogy, it is useful to review how they differ from modern, including modern Greek, theater.

The major distinctions fall into four categories. First, theater performance was a religious event, dedicated to

Dionysius, the deity associated with fertility in the narrow sense and more broadly the creative force that drives the continuity of life. For Greeks that life meant the community, or city-state. A formal procession in advance of the performance, culminating with the placing of a bust of Dionysius on an altar (*thymele*) in the arena (*orkestra*), assured his presence throughout the event. The plays themselves were tightly designed rituals originating at least two centuries earlier with the dithyramb, a celebration of Dionysius by priest and congregation chanting antiphonally. Because the actors had evolved from priests and were in effect functioning religiously, their bodies were regarded as sacrosanct. For that reason, murders (for example, Medea's of her children) were committed off-stage, and deaths were reported by messengers. As a consequence, there evolved a convention of eloquent messengers' reports to convey violent acts. And finally, because the event was a form of prayer for the community's continuity, historians speculate that probably the entire public attended, even women, children, and prisoners.

A further crucial distinction of ancient Greek theater from modern is the fact of the event as contest. Because a prize went to the winning trilogy according to a vote, dramatists predictably found ways to appeal to the crowd's civic and cultural pride. Most of the plots were familiar, and could not be departed from severely, but how so-and-so would handle such-and-such story this time was cause for suspense and honing of critical taste.

The prize was honorific rather than material, but competition was passionate, all within formalized rules for alternating scenes, dances, and use of the Chorus. Each dramatic poet submitted a trilogy followed by a short farcical satyr-play for relief. The government regularly commissioned a wealthy citizen for the privilege of financing productions. The plots of the trilogies being familiar, the dramatists' task was to render old material gripping by means of intense domestic conflicts and soaring language. Audiences might wonder, on hearing that Sophocles was about to present another *Antigone*, what treatment lay in store for them this time. These versions, of course, had to be limited to the plausible—for example, a story could not have Troy winning the war, or Medea dying a virgin.

The weightiest aspect of the contest framework was the fact that the winner was selected by a jury from the audience, with pressure from the crowd of up to 17,000 spectators. The comedies, too, which were performed at the festivals on other days, contained "pitches" for victory, but in keeping with the genre of comedy, they were far more blatant. Traditionally, one of the actors would step out of his role and declaim a direct appeal for the prize. Naturally, tribal preferences among the audience wielded influence, and claques or supporting groups made their passions heard. The greatest effect of the contest, however, was the challenge dramatists faced to design the content of their plays so as to flatter and elicit favor from the crowd and consequently the jury.

Physical factors mattered as well, aside from the statue of Dionysius. Song and dance, musical instruments, chiefly flute and drum, costumes and masks, all were part of theater's spectacle. The performance was outdoors in daylight, of course, and theaters were regularly situated so that audiences could observe throughout a performance, and Choruses could point to, both the wonders of nature in the distance and the achievements of the city-state nearby. The absence of any type of artificial lighting played a role in the content of the drama—another parallel with Shakespeare, in that words and gestures carried the burden of both settings during nighttime and the passage of time.

Finally, a marked distinction between ancient Greek and modern theater was the integral use of the Chorus. A group of twelve to fifteen men, portraying men and women—there were no women actors—singing, dancing, gesturing and pointing, came to serve a crucial set of purposes. They established mood and presented the driving situation/problem before the protagonist appeared—the plague, or miasma, for example, with which the Sphinx menaced Corinth—and they lyricized the drama with their song and dance.

Sometimes members of the Chorus participated more actively, interrogating, challenging, or agitating the protagonist, as with both kings Oedipus and Creon. In only one instance, in the second play of Aeschylus' trilogy, do they actually affect the action. But above all, by its nature as an anonymous group, the Chorus buffers the intensity at the center of the drama, and, incapable of heroic deeds itself (often slaves or old men or women), as often as not manifests the status quo against which the protagonist struggles, *agon* meaning struggle. Most critical, perhaps, is their demonstration of the public consequences of private (domestic) actions. Whatever their role, they always engaged in argumentation.

Ancient Greeks were apparently enamored of rhetoric, the use of language to persuade. And they grasped and apparently enjoyed its connection to democratic governance. Modern uses of the word "politics" range from ruthless vote-seeking to benign group dynamic, but for ancient Greeks persuasion was the key to governance, the name of which means navigation. The word "politics" comes from "polis," city-state or community, and then, as now, questions loomed about how to govern well. *Who* could be a citizen they decided in terms not very democratic by modern measure, but *how to behave* as a citizen was the compelling issue. And it had a great deal to do with rhetoric. Fifth-century B.C.E. Greeks knew that governance with citizen participation is all about the use of language to persuade.

It would be hard to overestimate the task that Aeschylus took on. In the first two plays of the trilogy, the *Agamemnon* and *Libation-Bearers* (*Choephoroi*), the grip of chthonic forces appears to be implacable. The primal revenge-driven Furies hound Queen Clytemnaestra even beyond the grave and make her son Orestes' life unbearable. The problem that the plays present is universal: how to deal with the killers of killers. Agamemnon had killed their daughter Iphigenia as a sacrifice to victory in the war against the Trojans; Clytemnaestra cannot allow that killing to go unavenged, so she kills Agamemnon; their son Orestes cannot allow the killing of his father to go unavenged, and so on, with what the Furies tellingly call "innocent murders."

Societies from time immemorial have operated under this obligation, and still do. Under the power of custom, each claim is justifiable. Clytemnaestra, for example, not only cites the death of Iphigenia; she makes the case before the Chorus-as-society that she is an instrument of retribution for her husband's many other wrongs, including bringing home from Troy a concubine princess. "Wipe out the man stained with murder," she exclaims. Her son as well needs to wipe out the murderer, his mother, of the murderer, his father. In the face of these colliding justifications and the resulting moral deadlock/dead-end, Aeschylus both proposed and reflected a new order that made possible the movement of the action to a very unlikely point of exultation. The instrument is Persuasion, the force to whom Athena defers (line 886) as she finally wins over the Furies.

Surely a primary legacy of Greek theater is the art of debate. Homer three centuries earlier had portrayed it, between enemies, between friends, and within oneself. People must have engaged in disputes from the time someone had to stake out a boundary. But in Greek tragedy we see dispute become central as a discipline that fostered the great philosophies that followed. Points of accusation and counter-accusation occur in staccato alternating lines (*stichomythia*, stitch-story), or in developed stanzas, now between main actors, now between one actor and the Chorus, who, themselves prevented from taking action, expose, sort out, and sharpen the issues.

Debate is the lifeblood of democracy. Argument, the marriage of passion and discourse, is a mode of getting to know. In Britain's Parliament, how like a serious tennis match is the back-and-forth articulation of positions. U.S. Supreme Court Justice Brandeis observed that the Constitution functions to prevent the arbitrary exercise of power. In a society where justice has no such safety-net, what recourse does one have against the arbitrary exercise of power? Sophocles' Antigone, though she justifies burying her brother against Creon's decree in the name of the gods, does not expect them to rescue her. As we discover, the gods hold her action as proper and Creon's denial of burial as wrong. But he has the political power, and she is armed only with a consuming conviction and a clear voice.

Like Antigone, Aeschylus's Prometheus in *Prometheus Bound* knows what he wants—loyalty to humankind—and is willing to sacrifice everything for it. But that dedication is not enough for the Greek audience. Prometheus, visited by a series of compromisers, has to speak the thrillingly persuasive selection and arrangement of words. Chained to a rock by the father of gods, Zeus, the oppressed Titan still has colossal power, that is, to make his case and keep alive the civilizing notion of doing so.

In the *Oresteia* Aeschylus both proposed and reflected. He proposed in giving artistic voice to a vision, yet he reflected because the notion had to be already in the public consciousness. Athenian society was ready to get unstuck from a primal vendetta pattern that had until then seemed perpetually inevitable.

On this point the contest factor of the trilogy weighs significantly. Unlike in modern drama, with individual reviewers, the playwright could not be too far behind or ahead of his audience—he was bound to its values and tastes by his desire to win its prize. Aeschylus had therefore observed and celebrated a new mind-set in Athens. In fact the year earlier, she had signed a peace treaty with Argos, where the story of Clytaemnestra and Agamemnon had begun, the home of the prince who throws himself at the mercy of Athens. This historical treaty indicated a mind-set that Aeschylus emblemized by transforming the horrific Eumenides ("kindly ones") from an ironic name to an actual benign force. He did this through his portrayal of Athena.

Athena, like most of the Olympians, bears many associations and is variously portrayed in classical stories. Ovid would show her, as Minerva, to be petty and viciously envious of the mortal weaver Arachne. Homer shows her as fiercely partisan to the Achaeans. She is the deity who deceives brave and honorable Hector into imagining that his brother Euphorbus has come to his side in battle against Achilles. (These disparities make clear the absurdity of Olympian biographies.) In the *Eumenides*, however, Athena is cloaked in judiciousness. Her questions and her judgments epitomize fairness. She is the only character in the play sensible enough to ask where all this bloodshed will finally lead.

This paragon of fairness is the patron deity of Athens, the city to which the action moves, via Delphi, from the Argos of the first two plays. This is where the audience of judges lives. To earn the prize, Aeschylus makes Athens enlightened in contrast with all those frozen in the hatred cycle. He clearly realized, however, that the powerful Furies and all the primal instincts they represent could not just be eradicated. The *Eumenides*, therefore, has everything to do with politics.

Aeschylus uses several devices to glorify the patron of Athens as admirably just. First, he uses Apollo, another Olympian deity familiar through Homer, as a foil to Athena. Apollo, defending Orestes in the second and third plays, had been responsible for goading the reluctant Orestes to murder his father. Too, the audience would recall from Homer that Apollo had supported the wife-abductor Paris (Alexander). His character threatens, bribes, speaks arrogantly, and uses irrational appeals, in contrast to Athena's logical and balanced rhetoric. For example, he reasons that Clytemnaestra's murder of her spouse was a more brutal violation than matricide. He also argues absurdly that a woman's role in bringing a child into the world is less important than a man's.

Despite Apollo's conspicuously flawed arguments of defense, though, Orestes has one defensible point: he has atoned. He has appealed as suppliant before the Oracle at Delphi and has arrived at Athens chastened, and, he believes, absolved. Is it possible that expiation under the new order may replace the old order's retribution? The case is thrown before Athena, with the spotlight removed from the personal issue of Orestes' guilt. He becomes a figure fought over rather than engaged in a fight.

Another device Aeschylus uses to glorify Athena is her discretion. With all the power handed to her, even by Apollo, she relinquishes authority to the community. If no single person (or god) can decide the case, she argues, because all personalities are hampered in judgment by some bias, she, too, is limited. The audience remembers that facing a domestic case, more precisely matricide, Athena, having sprung from Zeus's forehead, had no mother. She casts her ballot in favor of Orestes before the tribunal has voted. The outcome of their vote, a tie, is Aeschylus's strategy to accomplish two things, avoiding Orestes' all-or-nothing prognosis, and honoring the Furies, saving them from disgrace.

Aeschylus underscores Athena's acknowledgment of the Furies' authority—they could wield real power against the city. Their long plaintive resistance before accommodating to the new order shows the depth of their impulses. With utmost patience and diplomacy, Athena incorporates their primal outrage as a legitimate strength into the fabric of society, in service of civic order and arbitration—holding the community together.

As a means to endorse the new order over the old, Aeschylus in the *Eumenides* innovated a second Chorus to play judges, members of a tribunal, in the play within the play—a template for a favorable rendering by the audience's judges, There is indeed a place for moral outrage, the play asserts, but adjudication must not be personal—justice is a public responsibility.

What Aeschylus achieved was to dramatize an etiology of how that attitude, already viable in Athens' tribunals, might have originated on the Areopagitica, Mars Hill. The emergence of private vengeance into public justice would be a lesser story without the pageantry, the dance, the formal patterns, the spellbinding repetitions, celebrating the merger of instinct and civic authority, religion and patriotism, better than going to the beach. The savior in this drama is not Apollo, Zeus, or even Athena, but Persuasion, born and nurtured in the democratic city-state, and in return its lifeblood

How could Aeschylus not have won the prize?

Chapter Ten

Who or What Are the Greek Gods?

BY AND large the first association people make with the word "mythology" is Homer and the ancient Greek stories. His near-contemporary Hesiod, who also wrote extensively about the deities, hardly gets a mention. Narratives from the two Homeric epics occupy extravagant coffee-table books and highly colorful children's illustrated books. Courses in high school and college that deal with the subject of mythology begin with and seldom stray far from that body of images. What makes the Homeric stories particularly interesting as exemplary myths is that they are not exemplary myths. They have been worked over by and taken on the stamp of a supreme artist, who absorbed the society's traditional material and worked with it. Although the textual evidence leaves little doubt that Homer believed in the system, he shaped it according to his own design. Therefore his epics belong at the same time to an examination of sacred community stories and great art.

A leap of imagination is necessary in moving from

Western assumptions about religion to a respect for Greek theology of the ninth century B.C.E. The fundamental difference between the triad of Christianity, Judaism and Islam and the Greek system of belief is not merely monotheism as opposed to polytheism. Just as crucial is the fact that the Greeks did not suppose a personal relationship with the gods or worship them, any more than Native Americans worship the Coyote or Raven figures whose immense powers extend to having created humankind and the conditions around us. In many belief-systems in the world the word "god" signifies only an immortal being or supernatural personality, not the distillation within one personality of infinite knowledge (omniscience) and infinite power (omnipotence), that the three major monotheisms conceive of, a divinity infinitely engaged with our well-being.

As a result, polytheistic religions have no difficulty accounting for the problem of evil that confounds worshipers of a unique paradoxical deity who possesses absolute power, is favorably disposed toward—even invested in— the human race, and at the same time allows devastating suffering among them. Where would Western theodicy (accounting for the ways of God to man) be without Satan? The business of myths is to provide an accounting.

Recent discoveries reveal much about the well-kept secrets of the ancient Greek religious rites celebrated in Eleusis, a town near Athens regarded as holy in its connection with Demeter or Ceres (goddess of agriculture, chiefly grain, therefore fertility). The little we do know of these Eleusinian Mysteries reveals that worship of the forces behind the cycles of replenishing nature, embodied mostly in Demeter, the grieving mother of missing Persephone, satisfied the level of connectedness to the holy that the Olympian family never could.

Problems involved with applying the word "god" to the Greek deities can be allayed if one uses "immortal" in its place. It is, after all, deathlessness that distinguishes that set of characters from the human beings perpetually at risk of annihilation. Absorbing this fact, the reader/listener can better fathom Zeus's political role as chairman of the Olympian board, whose priority is to achieve accord. He cannot slay or even dismiss any of the group. He can only negotiate for peace among them, thus, as Homer demonstrates, serving as a model for a politic king.

How does the Olympian family of deities behave? When Zeus takes a fancy to a young mortal, Io, his consort Hera becomes jealous and tricks him into having Io transformed into a cow. Hera's envy leads her to numerous disguises and deceptions on mortal recipients of Zeus's amatory attentions, including Semele, mother of Dionysius. "Godly" dignity is not her province. Nor is it that of Aphrodite, who in the *Iliad* runs to her mother Dione for succor when she has interfered in the Trojan battlefield and had her hand wounded. Bleeding *ichor*, a facsimile of blood—a substance of no use for the deathless—she appears ridiculous in her whining imitation of mortals, who genuinely have something to fear. Food for the gods is also a facsimile; ambrosia means "not consumed or not consuming." The gods are ridiculous, though vividly delineated

Homer shows immortals on two levels of portraiture, specific, like the Olympians, and abstract, like Eris (Strife), Nemesis (Retributive Justice), and the three Fates—Clotho/Spinner, Lachesis/Disposer, and Atropos/Terminator. The abstract figures are easily recognizable icons of forces that mortals have perpetually to contend with. Eris, for example, is excluded from the marriage celebration by the parents of Achilles, future king of the Myrmidons. Who would invite

Strife to a wedding? But if she is dangerous when invited, she is far more dangerous when shunned. True to her nature, she causes great harm by introducing a contest among female deities that eventually leads to the ten-year Trojan War and widespread slaughter. When one searches for a cause of the war, it is not the competition among the three deities that Paris of Troy judges as Paris predictably would. Nor is it Paris's abduction of Menelaus's wife Helen, because that episode is merely one in a series of consequences of the wedding gaffe. For Homer, the cause of the war is the fact that Strife happens.

In Homer's own time and the earlier era he was writing about, a panic-stricken mother of an infant with a flaming fever would not turn to the Olympian deities. Most likely she would seek comfort and offer prayers—the universal impulse—at a local shrine where an accessible nature spirit on the order of the maternal Ceres was invited by villagers to reside. Practitioners, holy persons—another universal—whether they are successful or not, would be connected to the earth and not the remote heavens of Olympus. Two religions? Indeed. Today those in Japan who concurrently abide by the aboriginal Shintoism along with Taoism, Buddhism, and Confucianism find such compatibility unsurprising.

If the Olympian deities do not appear worship-worthy, what, then, was their function, those gods whose images come to us most completely in the epics Homer adapted and honed from traditional story material?

Homer uses the deities for two purposes. One is to present an orderliness to the cosmic system, a model that posits cogency and predictability in the face of the society's and individuals' uncertainty. The cosmos is peopled, not empty, not chaos. Human society, as always, had to deal with the anomalous welter of experience. The admirable Trojan

Hector knows he must face the greatest of all warriors, Achilles, and for a moment, thanks to a trick by Athena, he imagines one of his brothers coming to his aid. But when the image vanishes, he is left to confront his fears, and finally his bravery. Dramatizing the tension between doom and hope, Homer's narratives offer emotional, aesthetic, political and cosmological satisfaction.

A second purpose of the Olympian figures is to explore and glorify the tragic grandeur of humankind. When one tries to imagine living into infinity, one sees the futility of getting very far with that picture. What would it be like to live forever, to have forever? The Cumaean Sibyl was granted her wish for eternal life but neglected to ask for eternal youth, the result being that she shriveled down to a spider. Myth-tellers evidently enjoy the play of such conjectures.

When Ares/Mars, the deity identified with war, provokes Zeus beyond the point of endurance, what can the punishment be? Zeus confines him in a jar for two hundred years. Whatever his mischief, Ares is immortal, and so the story has to include his release, for the fact that war exists. No one could (yet) accept the death of war as true. That mere two-hundred-year instant of hiatus suggests how little the gods have at stake. Poor Aphrodite with her injured palm has eternity to heal or not heal. With nothing at stake, the gods are crucially different from us, despite their physical resemblance.

That incapacity to be at risk highlights the peril and courage of human beings, particularly heroes, and allows Homer to play with the idea of human glory. He portrays the immortals as imitating us in such rituals as hospitality, as if they had any corresponding bases for them. The extremes of hospitality in the Mediterranean world must have been grounded in practicality. There are at least four bases for it. A stranger might be a god testing one—Latona disguised as a parched crone turns a village into frogs, according to Ovid, when they deny her water she pleads for. Secondly, a stranger might turn out to be an emissary bearing important diplomatic or strategic information in this dangerous world. Thirdly, one would wish to have in turn a respectful reception of one's own emissary. The distances were so great and perilous from settlement to settlement that survival was close to a miracle.

Perhaps most of all, a traveler had a tale to tell — assuredly of the journey itself, as we see in Odysseus's hearty welcome in Scherie, and of other people and how they lived. Along with dance, song, and games, this news was a chief source of entertainment, of material for bards. And it provided education, what we might call today social studies, anthropology, geography, political science. It would be calamitous for people not to receive strangers well.

As for the gods, though, there could be none of these rewards. Their gestures of hospitality, therefore, like their *ichor* and *ambrosia,* are a hollow mimicry pointing out the limitations of their infinitude. Storytellers and listeners would naturally welcome portrayals of godly behavior that parallels ours—and yet does not. So the myths play upon similarities and distinctions, the essential distinction having to do with mortality.

Particularly but not exclusively through the figure of Achilles, Homer explores the dramatic power of foreknowledge of death. Achilles has been privileged to choose between an early glorious death and a long and undistinguished life. Choosing glory, he learns that his end will come after he has slain the Trojan Hector. In the poet Peter Viereck's words, he "wears death like dungarees." That is, he bears with excruciating consciousness the certainty that we all share but cannot afford to dwell on.

When the hero's pride, after humiliation by his commander-in-chief Agamemnon, delays his entry into battle, his conflict is palpable. He is assured by received notions—ancient Greek theology—so vastly different from modern Greek Orthodox Christianity, that the afterlife is an inescapably gloomy eternity, without the options immortals have to exercise personality. Armed with that knowledge, he chooses to make his life exciting and distinguished, to seize for himself the meaningfulness of glory in battle. It is not the Trojans who are his enemy, or his offending leader Agamemnon, but the fate that will steal everything from him except that one thing that he can control, the glory that will always attach to his name, as it still does.

Anyone who shares his fate, that is, all persons, may be able to understand this desire. Victor Frankl, a psychologist who survived Nazi death camps, has written about "man's search for meaning" as a greater impetus than survival, sex, nourishment, or other conjectured motivations.

But what can an immortal fathom of such needs? The three monotheisms embrace a god who is utterly wise, but the Olympian immortals are limited, they deceive, surprise and outwit one another. Even Chairman Zeus is stymied by the invulnerability of the misbehaving Olympians. Aside from the resourceful Athena, they have no particular gift for insight (Prometheus, whose name means foresight, and who delivered fire and therefore progress to human beings, was a Titan, not an Olympian, and limited in other ways). Homer depicts a kind of upstairs/downstairs division, in which the mortals, subject to the greatest of stakes when they go into battle, can be greatly admirable, while the gods can appear trivial.

For monotheists, this pettiness of the gods is often difficult to take seriously as religion. It denies the comforting certainties that their own religions offer. But within those monotheistic societies people still suffer and die, injustices still occur, and disaster strikes. The gods are not more or less effectual in protecting our lives, but the stories are accountings for a system that in itself offers a security. Zeus will always be Zeus, Ares Ares, Poseidon Poseidon. And death is always waiting at the end, offering human beings but not gods the opportunity for greatness and dignity.

Finally, a major misunderstanding of ancient Greek theology undervalues its sophistication. That is the notion that the gods determine fate, and we are their pawns. Nothing is farther from the truth about the role of the Olympians. A clearer grasp emerges when one considers the roles of Time and Ananke .

Here is how fate works in Homer's system. Once a certain event, say a home burning down, has taken place on a Tuesday afternoon, it must have had to have happened. But if one can be aware of it on Monday, it still will have to have happened on Tuesday. That awareness is not determinism. Rather it can make for tragedy, which is not possible for pawns.

The most trenchant point Homer makes is that the immortals are far more limited than mortals. Their unending time denies them any concept of tragedy or nobility. Moral significance has no relevance for them. Next to their triviality the sacrifices of mortals take on meaning. Hector at the wall reassuring Andromache and their little son with bravado as he goes off to engage with Achilles. King Priam's courage in his mission for his son's body, as his wife Hecuba warns that Achilles will tear out his liver. The poet's telegraphing the doom of Patroclus beforehand to underscore the pathos of his last minutes alive. The bravery of all warriors on the battlefield to defend their comrades' corpses and armor. All this in the face of the absolute cost, a death, as Achilles' ghost reports to Odysseus from the wisdom of afterlife, that is utterly abysmal. Homer has him tell his former comrade that he would now rather be a shepherd alive than a dead hero. That wisdom influences Odysseus to be more prudent.

The human choices, never the gods' choices, demonstrate dignity and worth.

And what of the plight of a captive who sets aside all goals but to survive? Whether one is to sacrifice life for honor or to endure another living day, neither the honor nor the endurance has meaning without the imminence of death. The exemption of the gods from such concerns marks them apart from humankind, and in Homer's cunning way diminishes them,

Gods cannot be heroes. Homer, while showing them to be potent in their deathlessness, at the same time celebrates human mortality and gives it magnitude. We have a span of time in which to define ourselves, he shows, within the imperatives of our conditions. Near the end of the *Odyssey*, Homer highlights the loyalty of an old family servant, as if to say that not only the illustrious get to make choices—we all do. But none of the gods do, because they do not have the privilege.

Bibliography

Aeschylus. *The Oresteia*. Translated by Robert Fagles. New York: Penguin, 1977.

________. *Oresteia,* Translated by Richard Lattimore. Chicago: University of Chicago Press, 1953.

________. *The Oresteian Trilogy,* Translated by Philip Vellacott. Baltimore: Penguin, 1962.

________. *Prometheus and Other Plays.* Editor, Philip Vellacott. Baltimore: Penguin, 1961.

Apollonius of Rhodes. *The Voyage of Argo.* Editor, E.V. Rieu. London: Penguin Books, 1971.

Baldry, H. C. *Ancient Greek Literature in its Living Context.* New York: McGraw-Hill, 1972.

Brown, Norman O. *Hermes the Thief: The Evolution of a Myth.* New York: Vintage, 1969.

Buckland, Raymond. *Witchcraft from the Inside.* St. Paul: Llewellyn Publications, 1971.

Bullfinch, Thomas. *Bullfinch's Mythology.* New York: The Modern Library, 1950.

Burrows, Lapides, Shawcross, Editors. *Myths and Motifs in Literature.* New York: The Free Press, 1973.

Burtt, E. A. Editor. *The Teachings of the Compassionate Buddha*. New York: New American Library, 1955.

Carpenter, Rhys. *Folk Tale, Fiction and Saga in the Homeric Epics*. Berkeley: University of California, 1962.

Christie, Anthony. *Chinese Myth*. Middlesex: The Hamlyn Publishing Group, 1968.

Clark-Kennedy, A.E., M. D. *The Art of Medicine in Relation to the Progress of Thought*. Cambridge: Cambridge University Press, 1945.

Coffin, Tristram P., Ed. *Indian Tales of North America*. Philadelphia: American Folklore Society, 1961.

Coulton, G. G. *The Medieval Scene*. Cambridge: The University Press, 1965.

Creel, H. G. *Chinese Thought: From Confucius to Mao Tse-Tung*. New York: New American Library, 1953.

Curtis, Vesta Sarkhosh. *Persian Myths*. Austin: British Museum Press, 1993.

Dalley, Stephanie., Translator. *Myths from Mesopotamia*. Oxford: Oxford University Press, 1991.

Daniel, Glyn E., et al. *Myth or Legend?* New York: Capricorn, 1968.

Dexter, Miriam Robbins. *Whence The Goddesses: A Source Book*. New York: Pergamon Press, 1990.

Dickinson, G. Lowes. *The Greek View of Life*. Ann Arbor: University of Michigan Press, 1958.

Eliade, Mircea. *The Sacred and the Profane: The Nature of Religion*. Translated by Willard R. Trask. New York: Harcourt, Brace, and World, 1959.

________. *The Quest: History and Meaning in Religion*. Chicago: University of Chicago, 1969.

________. *Myths, Dreams, and Mysteries*. New York: Harper and Row, 1960.

________. *Myth and Reality*. Translated by Willard R. Trask.

New York: Harper & Row, 1975.

______ . *The Myth of the Eternal Return.* Translated by Willard R. Trask. Princeton: Bollingen, 1974.

Feldmann, Susan. *The Story-Telling Stone: Traditional Native American Myths and Tales.* New York: Dell, 1965.

Finley M. I. *The World of Odysseus.* New York: The Viking Press, 1968.

Forsdyke, John. *Greece Before Homer.* New York: W. W. Norton & Company, 1964.

Frankfort, Henri, Mrs. H A. Frankfort, John A. Wilson, Thorkiljd Jacobsen. *Before Philosophy: The Intellectual Adventure of Ancient Man.* Baltimore: Penguin Books, 1961.

Gantt, W. Horsley, M. D. *Russian Medicine.* New York: Harper, 1937.

Gluckman, Max. *Politics, Law and Ritual in Tribal Society.* New York: New American Library, 1965.

Goodrich, Norma Lorre. *Medieval Myths.* New York: New American Library, 1961.

Gordon, R. K. *The Song of Beowulf.* London: J. M. Dent, [n.d.].

Grant, Michael. *Myths of the Greeks and Romans.* New York: New American Library, 1962.

________ . Translator. *Greek Literature: An Anthology.* Middlesex: Penguin, 1982.

Graves, Robert. *The Greek Myths, Volumes 1 and 2.* Baltimore: Penguin Books, 1955.

________. *The White Goddess.* New York: Farrar, Straus & Giroux, 1966.

Hamilton, Edith. *The Greek Way.* New York: Norton, 1930/1964.

________. *Mythology.* New York: Little, Brown, 1942.

Hesiod. *Theogony.* Translated, with an Introduction by Norman O. Brown. Indianapolis: The Bobbs-Merrill Company, 1953.

Hesiod. *Theogony & Works and Days.* Translated by M. L. West. Oxford: Oxford University Press, 1988.

Homer. *The Iliad.* Translated by Chase, Alston Hurd and William G. Perry, Jr. New York: Bantam, Books 1950.

________. *Odyssey.* Translated by Stanley Lombardo. Indianapolis: Hackett Publishing Company, 2000.

________. *The Odyssey.* Translated by Allen Mandelbaum. New York: Bantam Books, 1991.

________. *The Odyssey.* Translated by E. V. Rieu. Baltimore: Penguin Classics, 1956.

"Homeric Hymn to Demeter" in Watson, *The Road to Eleusis,* pages 69-83. Translated by Danny Staples.

Hooke, S. H. *Middle Eastern Mythology.* Baltimore: Penguin, 1966.

Hunningher, Benjamin. *The Origin of the Theater.* New York: Hill and Wang. 1961.

Huxley, Aldous. "The Perennial Philosophy." Introduction to *The Song of God: Bhagavad-Gita,* see below.

Jung, C. G. and C. Kerenyi. *Essays on a Science of Mythology.* Princeton: Bollingen, 1973.

Jung, C. G., Editor. *Man and His Symbols.* New York: Bantam Doubleday Dell, 1964.

Kitto, H. D. F. *Greek Tragedy.* London: Methuen, 1976.

_______ . The Greeks. Baltimore: Penguin 1962.

Kott, Jan. *The Eating of the Gods: An Interpretation of Greek* Tragedy. Translated by Boleslaw Taborski and Edward J. Czerwinski. New York: Vintage, 1974.

Kramer, Samuel Noah. *Mythologies of the Ancient World.* Garden City: Anchor, 1961.

Kroeber, Theodora. *The Inland Whale.* Berkeley: University

of California Press, 1929.

Liddell and Scott's Greek-English Lexicon. Oxford: Clarendon, 1966.

Malinowski, Bronislaw. *Magic, Science and Religion.* New York: Doubleday Anchor, 1954.

Mandel, Oscar. *A Definition of Tragedy.* New York: New York University Press, 1961.

Marriott, Alice and Carol K. Rachlin. *Plains Indian Mythology.* New York: New American Library, 1975.

May, Herbert G. and Bruce M. Metzger. *The Oxford Annotated Bible, Revised Standard Version.* New York: Oxford University Press, 1962.

Morris, William, ed. *The American Heritage Dictionary.* Boston: Houghton Mifflin, 1969.

Murray, Gilbert. *Five Stages of Greek Religion.* Garden City: Doubleday, 1955.

Murray, Henry A., ed. *Myth and Mythmaking.* New York: George Braziller, 1960.

O'Flaherty, Wendy Doniger, ed. *Hindu Myths.* Middlesex: Penguin, 1975.

Ovid. *The Metamophoses.* Translated by Horace Gregory. New York: Penguin, 1981.

Prabhavananda, Swami and Christopher Isherwood. *The Song of God: Bhagavad-Gita.* New York: New American Library, 1960.

Radin, Paul. *African Folktales.* New York: Princeton/Bollengen, 1970.

Raglan, Lord. *The Hero: A Study in Tradition, Myth, and Drama.* New York: Vintage, 1956.

Rank, Otto. *The Myth of the Birth of the Hero.* New York: Vintage, 1964.

Robertson, J. M. *Pagan Christs.* New Hyde Park: University Books, 1967.

Sandars, N. K. *The Epic of Gilgamesh*. Baltimore: Penguin, 1967.

Sewell, Richard B. *The Vision of Tragedy*. New Haven: Yale University Press, 1959.

Seznec, Jean, *The Survival of the Pagan Gods*. Translated by Barbara F. Sessions. New York: Harper/Bollingen, 1961.

Suzuki, D. T. *Zen Buddhism*. Edited by William Barrett. Garden City: Doubleday Anchor, 1956.

Thomas, D. Winton, ed. *Documents from Old Testament Times*. New York: Harper & Row, 1965.

Tyler, Hamilton A. *Pueblo Gods and Myths*. Norman: University Oklahoma, 1984,

Upanishads, The. Translated by Swami Prabhavananda and Frederich. Manchester. New York: New American Library, 1963.

Van der Post, Laurens. *The Lost World of the Kalahari*. Middlesex: Penguin Books, 1962.

Van Over, Raymond. *Sun Songs: Creation Myths From Around the World*. New York: New American Library, 1980.

Wasson, R. Gordon, with Albert Hofmann, Carl A. P. Ruck. *The Road To Eleusis: Unveiling the Secret of the Mysteries*. Berkeley: North Atlantic Books, 2008.

________. With Stella Kramrisch, Jonathan Ott, Carla P. Ruck. *Persephone's Quest: Entheogens and the Origins of Religion*. New Haven: Yale University Press, 1986.

Watts, Alan. *Myth and Religion in Chistianity*. London: Evergreen, 1960.

Wilhelm, Richard. European Commentary by C. G. Jung. *The Secret of the Golden Flower: A Chinese Book of Life*. London: Kegan Paul, Trench, Trubner & Co., 1932.

Whitman, Cedric H. *Homer and the Heroic Tradition.* New York: Norton, 1965.

Yohannan, John D., ed. *A Treasury of Asian Literature.* New York: New American Library, 1956.

Index

H

I

J

K

L

M

N

O

P

T

U

V

W

X

Y

Z